TEARFUL
MOMENTS
OF
RASULULLAH

TEARFUL MOMENTS OF RASULULLAH

First published in Malaysia by
Tertib Publishing
23-2 Jalan PJS 5/30
Petaling Jaya Commercial City (PJCC)
46150 Petaling Jaya, Selangor
Malaysia

Tel: +603 7772 3156

First Edition: November 2019

Cataloguing in-Publication Data is available from the National Library of Malaysia

ISBN: 978-967-17402-6-2

Cover design: Zahin Zulkipli | www.zahinzul.com
Transcription: Faslin Syarina Salim
Typesetting & Layout: Ainul Syuhada
Printed by: Firdaus Press Sdn. Bhd.

CONTENTS

Introduction

Bismillah

The aim of this short work, which grew from a series of lectures delivered by me 20 years ago in Texas, is to acquaint the believers with Muhammed Sala Allahu alayhi wa Sallam as the man he was. He, Sala Allahu alayhi wa Sallam, was not divine, nor immune to the stress and hardships we all face. He was, however, divinely inspired to lead a mandate of reform and righteousness within the self that begins with submission to the Omnipotent, Al-Mighty Allah, and extends outwardly to the betterment of all.

He loved us so much, sal Allahu alayhi wa sallam. He would think of those who would believe in him many generations after his generation and weep in longing and hope. He loved us more than some care to consider. Every Messenger of God was allowed a request that would be answered by Allah. All the Messengers utilised their invocation in the worldly life except for Muhammed, sal Allahu alayhi wa sallam. He, sal Allahu alayhi wa sallam, preserved his invocation to be intercession on the Day of Judgement for those who accept his message!

None can truly claim faith until Muhammed, sal Allahu alayhi wa sallam is more beloved to them than their parents, spouse and children. To know him is to love him. To love him is to obey him. If he, sal Allahu alayhi wa sallam, was to walk into your life now, what would he think?

I pray we can model the exalted behaviour of our Nabi Sala Allahu alayhi wa Sallam and that we are blessed with his intercession in the Day to come.

From a distance you notice his eyes – piercing, brilliant and engaging. The choicest Praise and Mercy of Allah be upon him. Muhammed, the Praised one is Ahmed, the greatest in Praise of Allah; sublimely appropriate. Al-Mustapha, the Divinely Chosen, is real. He was flesh and blood. Human.

I love him, O Allah, I love him sal Allahu alayhi wa sallam.

In a world of distortion, where truth is overcome by fiction, the full moon rises. Although obscured by shadows or an overcast sky, the moon remains. Such is the fame and honour of Muhammed, sal Allahu alayhi wa sallam.

Of average height, he towers above the elite of history. He would stand fully erect without a lazy slump. He was powerful, sal Allahu alayhi wa sallam. His chest was broad with a dusting of hair that extended vertically in a thin line down to his flat stomach, sal Allahu alayhi wa sallam.

Any kind of hardships you can envision and pray to never face was shouldered by him, sal Allahu alayhi wa sallam, simultaneously.

He experienced in his 63 years of blessed life more tribulation than a cohort. He, sal Allahu alayhi wa sallam, was an orphan, a widower, battle scarred, and unjustly outcast. He outlived many of his children and buried some of his grandchildren. His uncle, the Mercy of Allah be upon him, was martyred and his body desecrated. He, sal Allahu alayhi wa sallam, was defamed, mocked, lied to and lied about. He was poisoned, stoned, and had to witness his companions tortured on account of their faith in his Message, sal Allahu alayhi wa sallam.,

Sabraan, remain steadfast in patience, O Family of Yasser; your destination is Paradise. His teaching was simple. Allah, the All Mighty, is the only One deserving of worship and devotion. All that we encounter is by His Command. No harm can befall without His Permission.

His hair, sal Allahu alayhi wa sallam, was black and wavy. He liked to keep it longer in length, usually not past his earlobes. It contained a few gray strands, about 23 in number. With dark irises he could, by Divine Permission, view a world that was unseen. He had long, dark eyelashes that from a distance could be mistaken for kohl. He, sal Allahu alayhi wa sallam, would not avert his attention from a petitioner until their voice fell silent. His eyes would sleep but his heart was awake. His eyes never betrayed or invited treachery, sal Allahu alayhi wa sallam.

The weakest, poorest and socially downtrodden would access him, sal Allahu alayhi wa sallam, as readily as the chieftains. He sheltered the needy, fed the hungry, protected the vulnerable, guarded the secrets and instructed the uninformed. He, sal Allahu alayhi wa sallam, was calm when others were agitated, loving when others were filled with hate, and polite when shown contempt. He, sal Allahu alayhi wa sallam, is the highest standard of character and the spring of Divinely ordained etiquette.

His skin, sal Allahu alayhi wa sallam, was soft and naturally fragrant. His blessed hands were softer than silk and gave off the scent of aromatic musk. He was reddish in colour. He was not dark, nor was he pale. His skin was blemished with the seal of prophethood between his shoulder blades. He was proportional in all respects, sal Allahu alayhi wa sallam.

In his prayer, he found comfort and pleasure. His voice quivered in awe of the All Mighty. When leading others, he would, for the most part, recite from al-Qisar (the short chapters). If he heard a child crying, he would cut the recitation short to relieve the parent of any distress. His, sal Allahu alayhi wa sallam, grandchildren would ride atop his back during his prostration, and he would not move until they felt content. His voice was measured, and he paused at the end of every verse. He would recite the Quran in various accents to accommodate all the dialects of his companions. When alone at night, he would pray. He would remain vigilant for half the night, sometimes more, sometimes less. When he recited a passage addressing Allah's Divine Mercy, he would stop and ask for it. If one of torment, he would seek protection from it, sal Allahu alayhi wa sallam.

His face, sal Allahu alayhi wa sallam, was manifest beauty. His eyes were well set apart and covered by full brows. They were not sunk into his face or overtly protruding. His mouth smelled sweet, and his teeth were always clean and white. His saliva was a medicine and blessing, sal Allahu alayhi wa sallam. By the Grace of Allah, it was a cure to the blind, increase in food to the poor, and an ointment to the disfigured. He had a full, dark beard that obscured his slender long neck from a distance. His smile was radiant, sal Allahu alayhi wa sallam.

He was soft spoken except when he sermonised on Friday. His voice was melodious and captivating. He spoke only when necessary and refrained from idle chit-chat. His, sal Allahu alayhi wa sallam, tongue was true. He loved to listen and would ask questions of those whom he instructed. He was modest and sensitive to the needs and feelings of others. He smiled and laughed often, seldom loudly.

When he, sal Allahu alayhi wa sallam, was displeased, it could be read from his face. He never raised his hand against another living creature except during Divinely ordained battle. He, sal Allahu alayhi wa sallam, was courageous and led from the forefront. He stood in the ranks of his soldiers and faced the hardship they endured. He ate what they ate, slept where they slept and dressed as they dressed. He, sal Allahu alayhi wa sallam, was a man unlike the world has ever seen.

He, sal Allahu alayhi wa sallam, dressed similar to his compatriots. He never owned a throne or regal markings to distinguish himself, sal Allahu alayhi wa sallam, from others. He would walk without an escort and disliked sentries being placed to guard him. He preferred neutral shades of white, green and black to clothe himself with. When he ate, it was never to his fill, and he always ate while sharing his food with others. He loved milk, dates and honey. His favourite dish was tharrid – roasted mutton on buttered bread and broth.

He, sal Allahu alayhi wa sallam, cared for the earth and despised wastefulness and corruption. He was a tree hugger LITERALLY. He loved animals and instructed his companions to show kindness to them. When a camel wept, he would stroke it and speak to it in hushed tones. When the tree whimpered, he paused his sermon and embraced its trunk, whispering to it soothing words of comfort. Animals took comfort in him, sal Allahu alayhi wa sallam.

Today, his modality of life and tradition remain intact, preserved not only in print, but in conscious spirit.

I pray that the lessons found in this simple, but important retelling of moments of happiness & sorrow, tears, pain & comfort experienced by our Nabi sal Allahu alayhi wa sallam will lead us to reflect upon our own life.

In every hadith to be studied are numerous lessons to be gleamed and reflected upon. The Sunnah is relevant. Muhammed sal Allahu alayhi wa sallam is relevant.

O you who believe, send your greetings to Muhammed, sal Allahu alayhi wa sallam.

Yahya Ibrahim

CHAPTER 1

TEARFUL MOMENTS OF THE PROPHET'S LIFE

Prophet Muhammad [peace and blessings be upon him] was a normal human being in many respects, but who was chosen and that is why one of his names is AlMustafa (the chosen one).

Prophet Muhammad [peace and blessings be upon him] was chosen by Allah at the time when there was no heart that was greater in purity, greater in sanctity, greater in love and mercy than his heart. There are numerous hadiths that allude to this fact that Allah Subhanahu wa Ta'ala, as The Prophet [peace and blessings be upon him] says, "He looked to the people of the earth at that time and He saw that there was no cleaner heart than the heart of Muhammad." And Allah looked to the heart of the people once again and saw that the most pure of heart were those of the sahabah who would eventually be chosen by Allah Subhanahu wa Ta'ala to be the companions of Prophet Muhammad [peace and blessings be upon him].

We are going to be studying some of the most painful moments in the life of Rasulullah [peace and blessings be upon him]; some of the moments that were of the greatest weakness of the ummah; moments of The Prophet's [peace and blessings be upon him] personal tragedies; moments where he was moved to tears due to the influences of others, due to his love for his ummah, due to the situation that he found himself in or instances that arose in his leadership of the Muslim ummah.

In studying this, it brings us greater clarity of the personality of Rasulullah [peace and blessings be upon him]. When we come to see Prophet Muhammad [peace and blessings be upon him] in these tearful moments, in these moments of weakness and sorrow, we come to find greater love for Rasulullah [peace and blessings be upon him].

Prophet Muhammad [peace and blessings be upon him] lived a distinguish life. He lived a life that was for Allah, in the pursuit of Allah Subhanahu wa Ta'ala, and in the leadership of those who wished to come towards their Creator, Allah The Most Noble and The Most Merciful.

Therefore, it is important for us to study the sunnah of The Messenger [peace and blessings be upon him] by looking at his life, not just in terms of the written or the oral transmission of the hadiths, but rather to see how these instances shaped his life and therefore shape the life of the ummah that would come after him.

InshaAllah, in the next chapters, we will read a series of six or seven different discussions regarding pivotal moments, the different ahadith that are collected in the authentic traditions of The Prophet [peace and blessings be upon him], in the books of AlBukhari, Muslim, Abu Daud, Tirmidhi, AnNasa`i, and Ibn Majah. We will take these ahadith and look at these tearful moments or these moments of sorrow, and analyse how the ummah is to benefit from it and how The Prophet [peace and blessings be upon him] used them as a measure of instruction to those who were around him, and therefore the rest of the ummah that would come after him.

For each of the section, we will study two or three different hadiths, we will look at who the sahabah involved were – a short biography of them; who is Abdullah ibn Mas'ud, who is Umar ibn AlKhattab, how was this relevant to them – the circumstances of the happening, what is the context of this particular hadith, what is the context of the situation that involved in it, and what are the fiqh points that the scholars have extracted from all of these particular hadiths.

Therefore, it is a mighty, multidimensional study of this particular tearful moments and moments of sorrow from the life of Prophet Muhammad [peace and blessings be upon him].

WHAT IT MEANS TO BE A MESSENGER

None of us are going to experience prophethood or messengership. But we need to understand what is the role that the messenger and the prophet played, in order to understand how these moments later on – that would be experienced by Prophet Muhammad [peace and blessings be upon him] – are life-changing and ummah-changing events.

First, we look at these two terms that we are all very familiar with from our readings of the Quran and the hadiths, and the sermons that we hear. What is a prophet? When we study the word *Nabi*, it means and it comes from the root of *naba*. *Naba* means to inform or to give knowledge. Therefore, we read the first two verses of surah An-Naba, the translation says, "About what are they asking one another? About the great news -" The word *naba* is used in verse two.

Hence, a prophet is someone who gives information that he has been informed of from a source that is unknown to the others. It is knowledge that is given to him through revelation by Allah Subhanahu wa Ta'ala. There are many places in the Quran where we find that Allah Subhanahu wa Ta'ala mentions to Prophet Muhammad [peace and blessings be upon him] using the word "inform". For example, in surah Al-Hijr, verses 49 and 50, the translation says, "Inform my servants that it is I who am The Forgiving, The Merciful. And that it is My punishment which is the painful punishment."

The second word is *rasul* or messenger. A messenger is different than a prophet. The scholars have come to term with this. In the Arabic linguistic sense, a rasul is someone who is given a message to deliver. Therefore, if I were to ask one of the brothers to deliver a message to the sisters, that person becomes my messenger. From this, we could see the difference between knowing knowledge and teaching it, and being someone who is dedicated with the particular trait and a particular discipline that one is ordered and instructed to teach.

Regarding the woman who ruled the people at the time of Prophet Sulaiman [peace be upon him], when she was informed of a letter coming from Prophet Sulaiman [peace be upon him] asking her to submit to Allah, she responded as mentioned in surah An-Naml, verse 35, the translation says, "But indeed, I will send to them a gift and see with what (reply) the messenger will return." The word *almursalun* used in this verse means as a messenger, or an envoy, or as an ambassador. That is the linguistic usage of the word rasul.

However, we learn that a rasul is someone who has been given a specific instruction by Allah Subhanahu wa Ta'ala.

The Difference Between the Prophets and the Messengers

The prophets are those who were given the message of people who came before them. We find that Zakariya, Yahya, and Isa [peace be upon them] were all prophets at the same time under the leadership of the Taurah that was given to the rasul, Musa [peace be upon him]. They were ordered to maintain the traditions and the laws of Musa [peace be upon him]. Yahya and Zakariya [peace be upon them] were prophets upon the tradition of Musa [peace be upon him].

Then Isa [peace be upon him] came. He was different from Yahya and Zakariya [peace be upon them] because he was given an Injil, a new revelation. So, he had the transmission and he was ordered to give the new instruction of the new laws, as Allah Subhanahu wa Ta'ala says in surah Ali Imran, verses 50 and 51.

Isa [peace be upon him] says as part of his mission is to make halal (permissible) for the people some of the things that the Taurah has made haram (impermissible). There were certain things that the Taurah in its dietary laws, financial practice laws; all of the things that were very stringent and they were the laws that were given to Musa [peace be upon him]. Isa [peace be upon him] came at the time where there was to be a new instruction.

Therefore, we have an underlying principle. A messenger is one whom Allah Subhanahu wa Ta'ala has revealed to him a new system of governance and laws. Meanwhile, the prophets are those who came to revitalise the laws that were sent to those who came before them. Thus, we find that there is the third segment of the prophets and messengers; those who were both prophets and messengers. Initially they came as a prophet. But due to the corruption of the land and the exaggeration that Bani Israil had done in transforming the Taurah from its original, Allah

Subhanahu wa Ta'ala brought down a new legislation, which is the Injil to Isa [peace be upon him].

So there are those who are prophets as in an authentic hadith narrated by Imam Ahmad, Prophet Muhammad [peace and blessings be upon him] said that there are 124,000 prophets that were sent to mankind. From those 124,000 there were 315 or slightly more messengers. The scholars of Islam agreed that every messenger began as a prophet. Every messenger is a prophet, but it is not necessary for every prophet to be a messenger.

After we understand these two terms, it will be important for us to understand the role of Prophet Muhammad [peace and blessings be upon him] as we will see he came down to follow the laws as Isa [peace be upon him] has proclaimed in the Injil. It is recorded for us in the Quran that Prophet Muhammad [peace and blessings be upon him] came to the people and said to them, "I have come to you with the same spirit of that which is found in the Injil, with the same laws as that which is found in the Taurah. Very little dispute or different between the rules and regulations of our traditions and that of the People of Book."

The Duties of the Prophets and the Messengers

It is important for us to see the seven distinct duties that the prophets and messengers are ordered to fulfil, so that we will see how each of these seven comes to play in the tearful moments of the life of Prophet Muhammad [peace and blessings be upon him].

 ## Conveyance of knowledge

The first and most important duty is the conveyance of knowledge. The transmission of what they have been informed with to give it to those who they are instructed to lead. Allah Subhanahu wa Ta'ala says in surah Al-Maidah verse 67, the translation says, "O Messenger, announce that which has been revealed to you from your Lord, and if you do not, then you have not conveyed His message; and Allah will protect you from the people; indeed, Allah does not guide the disbelieving people."

Therefore, the prophets are ordered to perform conveyance of knowledge in a clear light. Here we can see the importance of the sunnah of Prophet Muhammad [peace and blessings be upon him]. In surah Al-Kahf verse 27, Allah says, "And recite (O Muhammad) what has been revealed to you of the Book of your Lord; there is no changer of His words, and never will you find in other than Him a refuge."

In fulfilling this obligation, Prophet Muhammad [peace and blessings be upon him] can simply transmits to the sahabah the letter for letter, the word for word, the verse for verse of the Quran. But in doing just the simple oral transmission does not fulfil the obligation of conveyance of the knowledge. Therefore, Allah Subhanahu wa Ta'ala says to him in surah An-Nahl verse 44, "(We sent them) with clear proofs and written ordinances; and We have brought down to you the reminder so that you may make clear to the people what was sent down to them and that they might give thought." Before that, Allah Subhanahu wa Ta'ala mentions to us in surah Al-Baqarah verse 151, "Just as We have sent among you a messenger from yourselves reciting to you Our verses ..."

It is crucial for us to understand the first and most important duty of Prophet Muhammad [peace and blessings be upon him] is to transmit everything stated and to show its practice in its proper form, which is the tradition and the sunnah of the Prophet [peace and blessings be upon him].

We conclude this point by the word of Aisha [may Allah pleased with her] where when she was asked to describe Prophet Muhammad [peace and blessings be upon him], she said, "It was as if he was the Quran walking amongst the people." Everything that he did, everything that he said in one way or another led back to the words of Allah.

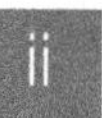 ## Calling towards Allah

The second duty of the prophets is calling towards Allah. It is insignificant simply just to say, "These are the words of Allah" and not call others towards Him. Prophet Muhammad [peace and blessings be upon him] and those who follow in his practice invite people towards Allah. In other word, doing da'wah. Da'wah means to call, to show the reality so that people will become enticed by this particular discussion and particular belief that you have.

Allah Subhanahu wa Ta'ala says in surah An-Nahl verse 36, the translation says, "And We certainly sent into every nation a messenger (saying), 'Worship Allah and avoid Taghut'; and among them were those whom Allah guided, and among them were those upon whom error was (deservedly) decreed; so proceed through the earth and observe how was the end of the deniers."

Taghut is anything that is worshipped and glorified in the way that only Allah Subhanahu wa Ta'ala should be.

In surah Al-Anbiya verse 25, Allah Subhanahu wa Taala says, "And We sent not before you any messenger except that We revealed to him that, 'There is no deity except Me, so worship Me.'"

"Be mindful of Allah and obey Him" has been stated by all of the prophets in the different transmissions that we have found in the Quran. For example, in surah Ash-Shu'ara verse 110. This is the famous statement of all of the different prophets, such as Lut, Nuh, and Ibrahim [peace be upon them] as well as Muhammad [peace and blessings be upon him].

 Bring good news and give warning

Prophet Muhammad [peace and blessings be upon him] and all of the messengers were ordered to perform the task of bringing good news and giving a warning.

About the descriptive terms of Prophet Muhammad [peace and blessings be upon him], Allah Subhanahu wa Ta'ala describes him as in surah Al-Ahzab verses 45 to 48, "O Prophet, indeed We have sent you as a witness and a bringer of good tidings and a warner. And one who invites to Allah, by His permission, and an illuminating lamp. And give good tidings to the believers that they will have from Allah great bounty. And do not obey the disbelievers and the hypocrites but do not harm them, and rely upon Allah; and sufficient is Allah as Disposer of affairs."

In the above verse, it is mentioned that The Prophet [peace and blessings be upon him] is a witness, a bringer of good news, a warner to mankind, a caller towards Allah, and a brilliant amber of light that people can be guided by.

Allah Subhanahu wa Ta'ala says in surah Al-Kahf verse 56, the translation says, "And We send not the messengers except as bringers of good tidings and warners; and those who disbelieve dispute by (using) falsehood to (attempt to) invalidate thereby the truth and have taken My verses, and that of which they are warned, in ridicule."

The syntax is very important. You do not find Allah Subhanahu wa Ta'ala mentioning of a warner before a giver of good news. It is from the characteristics of the one calling to Allah to make things simple for the people – to give them hope, to give them a desire to do further good deeds. It is more important to do good than it is to stay away from evil. Think of this concept. As Muslims, we are taught by the Prophet [peace and blessings be upon him] and we are taught through his sunnah that it is more important to perform al-ma'roof than it is to stay away from al-munkar. Not that that diminishes from the importance of staying away from things that are prohibited.

The reason we are asked by Allah Subhanahu wa Ta'ala to do good is because the more good you do, the more of an inspiration or a conviction built in you to stay away from the evil. Numerous instances in the life of Prophet Muhammad [peace and blessings be upon him] and the sahabah show that a person would be in a state of sin, but when you would fulfil the act of worship and the act of righteousness, it would help to overcome the difficulties that you face that led you away from Allah Subhanahu wa Ta'ala.

Thus, the role of a prophet is a person who gives good instructions – fills the heart of the believers with hope and love for Allah Subhanahu wa Ta'ala – and equally as well as a warner.

 Perform purification of the souls of those who follow them with tazkiyah

They bring about a rectification of a person's being. They change a person's life from evil to good. Almost instantaneously.

We see numerous examples of this from the life of Prophet Muhammad [peace and blessings be upon him]. A person would come to him seeking to harm him and within an instant you hear this person has entered into the faith of Islam.

For example, the story of Umar ibn AlKhattab [may Allah be pleased with him] who was seeking ill-intent in his heart. He wanted nothing more than to end the life of Muhammad [peace and blessings be upon him]. However, when he went to his sister's home and he heard just one or two verses from surah Taha , it filled him with belief. The verse from the Quran changed his life.

There is also the example of Khalid ibn AlWalid. He was one of the most instrumental people before his Islam in the lost that the Muslims suffered during the Battle of Uhud. But yet when he heard the word from Prophet Muhammad [peace and blessings be upon him], he submitted himself to Rasulullah and to the way of Allah.

When the pagans from different cities came to perform their pre-Islamic hajj (hajj of jahiliyya), the mushrikin would say to them, "Put cotton in your ears so that you do not hear the words of Muhammad. Because if you hear them, they will cause you to leave your wife, and your children will abandon you." That was the type of hysteria that was built around the words of Prophet Muhammad [peace and blessings be upon him] and the fear that they had of the truth entering into their heart.

So we find the words of Prophet Muhammad [peace and blessings be upon him], the words of the Quran, and his traditions had a profound effect on people. They brought rectification and tazkiyah. They change the life and the conditions of people for the better.

In the translation of surah Ash-Shura verses 52 and 53, Allah Subhanahu wa Ta'ala says, "And thus We have revealed to you an inspiration of Our command; you did not know what is the Book or (what is) faith, but We have made it a light by which We guide whom We will of Our servants; and indeed, (O Muhammad) you guide to a straight path. The path of Allah, to whom belongs whatever is in the heavens and whatever is on the earth; unquestionably, to Allah do (all) matters evolve."

As stated in the Quran, Prophet Muhammad [peace and blessings be upon him] recited to us from the words of Allah, which we translate as, "Allah is The Waliy (The Protector, The Friend, The Aide) of those who have faith in Him; He extracts them out of the many shades of darkness into the one shade of the brilliance of light ..." That is a profound parable that Allah Subhanahu wa Ta'ala mentions to us. It also shows us that a person can have many different levels of darkness, but when the guidance of Allah comes to him and his heart is blessed with the light of faith, he can see clearly around him.

For this reason, Prophet Muhammad [peace and blessings be upon him] was given the label by Allah Subhanahu wa Ta'ala as *Sirajan Munira*. A siraj is a brilliant light, an amber, a flame that can be seen from many distances. It can be seen through the many different stages of darkness. Its light is unchanging in its power. And that is the message of Muhammad [peace and blessings be upon him].

"And We certainly sent Musa with Our signs, (saying), 'Bring out your people from darknesses into the light and remind them of the days of Allah', and indeed in that are signs for everyone patient and grateful." Surah Ibrahim, verse 5.

The prophets and messengers were always instructed by Allah as Allah says in the verse mentioned above.

In surah Al-Haj from verse 46, Allah says, "... for indeed, it is not eyes that are blinded, but blinded are the hearts which are within the chests." It is the heart that is unaware of the true nature, unaware of its true purpose in this life, unaware of the soul, and unaware what it is required to perform towards Allah Subhanahu wa Ta'ala.

"But they worship rather than Allah that which does not benefit them or harm them, and the disbeliever is ever, against his Lord, an assistant (to satan). And We have not sent you (O Muhammad), except as a bringer of good tidings and a warner." Surah Al-Furqan, verses 55 and 56.

In the above verses of surah Al-Furqan, Allah describes these types of people who have sight but cannot see, who have hearing but cannot hear, and who have a heart but cannot understand. They worship other than Allah and they are in conflict on what Allah has ordered, what has of no benefit to them, and what cannot harm them. At times a person will be compelled to obey someone not because he will benefit, but because he is afraid of the harm.

Here Allah Subhanahu wa Ta'ala says that the things they worship are of no benefit and equal they are of no harm to them. So there is a waste of this worship that should be solely dedicated to Allah Subhanahu wa Ta'ala. Therefore, we see the dua of Ibrahim and other prophets [peace be upon them all] calling for Muhammad [peace and blessings be upon him] as the final messenger.

"Our Lord, and send among them a messenger from themselves who will recite to them Your verses and teach them the Book and wisdom and purify them; indeed, You are the Exalted in Might, the Wise." Surah Al-Baqarah, verse 129.

V   Unifying the proper mode of thought

Bringing about a true philosophy or understanding of the nature of things and the order of things. Also, to bring about the true understanding of aqeedah – understanding of the worship of Allah Subhanahu wa Ta'ala and what it means to believe.

Allah says mankind at one point in time before Nuh [peace be upon him], gathered together as one nation; did not matter what language, what color, what race.

"Mankind was (of) one religion (before their deviation); then Allah sent the prophets as bringers of good tidings and warners and sent down with them the Scripture in truth to judge between the people concerning that in which they differed; and none differed over the Scripture except those who were given it – after the clear proofs came to them – out of jealous animosity among themselves; and Allah guided those who believed to the truth concerning that over which they had differed, by His permission, and Allah guides whom He wills to a straight path." Surah Al-Baqarah, verse 213.

These people were gathered upon other than worship of Allah, so Allah was compelled and sought to send for us as human beings messengers and prophets who will give us glad tidings and warners of the evil that we may have fallen into.

Ibn Kathir and other scholars of Islam gave us very poignant discussions regarding this verse. They say it is the nature of a human being – due to the promise of shaytan who said, "I will do my best to misguide them and I will come to them from their right and from their left, from before them and from behind them, and I will leave non of them except until they disobey and are disbelievers in You." But Allah Subhanahu wa Ta'ala has made a covenant with mankind from before our existence that we will believe in Allah, we will worship Him, and we will follow the Messenger [peace and blessings be upon him]. Those of us who accepted had been led to the guidance of Allah 'Azza wa Jalla.

It is important for us to understand that there are two things that lead us away from Allah. Everything in life that leads us away from Allah has one of these two roots: Doubt and desire. These are the two reasons that mankind have within them that lead us away from Allah Subhanahu wa Ta'ala, if we do not seek to come towards Allah.

In many places in the Quran, Allah says, "Allah leads you to the place where you choose. Either you will be thankful or ungrateful." The one who is grateful to Allah is the believer, meanwhile the one who is ungrateful to Allah Subhanahu wa Ta'ala have left the way of Islam. There is no compulsion in the matter of faith or religion; the one who wishes to believe, let him believe and the one who wishes to be ungrateful and enter into kufr, let him be ungrateful and enter into kufr.

The nature of a human being is that he has been given these choices by Allah Subhanahu wa Ta'ala and people at a point in time before Nuh [peace be upon him], gathered upon kufr. So the balance that brings back humanity towards the worship of Allah are the prophets and the messengers. That is why it took the greatest prophet and the greatest messenger to be final prophet to countermeasure all of the kufr and all of the shirk that will later happen in his ummah.

Think of it in this way. That for every ummah, to counterbalance the sins of the people, Allah would have to send messengers and prophets. Bani Israil, at one point in time would have not one, nor two, nor three, but ten prophets. We see all of the kufr and shirk that may be found within the lands around the world. We know that there is no messenger and prophet coming after Muhammad [peace and blessings be upon him]. And that shows you the greatness of Rasulullah [peace and blessings be upon him]. This one man and this tawheed that he was given counterbalances all of the sins that we see, we experience, and we hear. He was sent to us to give us the upright way, the deen of Ibrahim [peace be upon him].

Thus, one of the missions of the prophets is to lead people to the correct understanding.

VI — A proof and evidence

The prophets and messengers are the proof of burden, a proof against and for mankind in terms of the laws of Allah Subhanahu wa Ta'ala.

"(We sent) messengers as bringers of good tidings and warners so that mankind will have no argument against Allah after the messengers; and ever is Allah Exalted in Might and Wise." Surah An-Nisaa, verse 165.

Allah Subhanahu wa Ta'ala has sent for the people multitude of messengers as givers of good news and warners, so that mankind cannot come later on and say, "We did not receive evidence and proofs from Allah". That will be the first hadith that we study from the tearful moments of Prophet Muhammad [peace and blessings be upon him], where he comes to recognize that the weigh of the ummah is upon his shoulders. He is the one who will be a witness over all of the ummah of Islam, from his moment until the Day of Judgement. This brings him calling towards Allah 'Azza wa Jalla.

"And if We had destroyed them with a punishment before him, they would have said, 'Our Lord, why did You not send to us a messenger so we could have followed Your verses before we were humiliated and disgraced?' Say, 'Each (of us) is waiting; so wait, for you will know who are the companions of the sound path and who is guided.'" Surah Taha, verses 134 and 135.

In the above verses, Allah Subhanahu wa Ta'ala has shown that the message of Islam shall enter into every home. In every place at one point or another, people will come to hear the words of Muhammad [peace and blessings be upon him] and the message of Islam. This was mentioned in an authentic hadith.

Allah Subhanahu wa Ta'ala says in surah An-Nahl verse 89, the translation says, "And (mention) the Day when We will resurrect among every nation a witness over them from themselves; and We will bring you (O Muhammad), as a witness over your nation; and We have sent down to you the Book as clarification for all things and as guidance and mercy and good tidings for the Muslims."

Before the death of Prophet Muhammad [peace and blessings be upon him], in his final khutbah in Arafah, he said, "O Allah, witness that I have conveyed the knowledge." And then he pointed to the heaven and pointed down to the people gathered with him.

Allah brought down the verses in surah Al-Maidah, regarding the completion of the faith of Islam. In verse 3 of the surah, Allah says, "... This day I have perfected for you your religion and completed My favor upon you and have approved for you Islam as religion; but whoever is forced by severe hunger with no inclination to sin, then indeed Allah is Forgiving and Merciful."

vii Leaders of nations

It is important for us to know that Islam is not simply just a religion that seeks to have individuals in the mosques, praying, fasting, and leaves other needs in life. This is one of the negative effects that we find in our time today.

Part of the effect of modernism is that the people who began to govern Muslim land said to the religious leaders, "You stay in the mosque, and you teach people Quran and hadith. Leave things like politics, military, war, and ethics to us." This cause separation of ideologies. To this day, we can still see the effect. We will find that in certain places, the people who are the most out of touch with what is happening in the world are the people who were given the most important admonitions to the Muslim. They have lost touch in certain aspects of what is truly happening.

However, this was never the case for the Prophet [peace and blessings be upon him]. We learn that he was involved in all aspects of the worldly life and spiritual life. He would take the opinions of the sahabah in matters of war – for example, the Battle of Khandaq. The Prophet [peace and blessings be upon him] would speak about economics and about the rights – who have more right to the land or right to the water? Everything was sent to him.

"O Daud, indeed We have made you a successor upon the earth, so judge between the people in truth and do not follow (your own) desire, as it will lead you astray from the way of Allah; indeed, those who go astray from the way of Allah will have severe punishment for having forgotten the Day of Account." Surah Sad, verse 26.

In the above verse, Allah Subhanahu wa Ta'ala has also said to Prophet Daud [peace be upon him], "We have made you someone who is ruling on earth as a representative of those who came before you. Give rules amongst people with the truth that has been sent to you." All of the prophets and the messengers have this duty. It was not just simply leading the prayers and reciting the Quran; but it was instructions, laws, military, economics, everything came into the life of the prophets and the ummah.

With this, we conclude our introduction to the role of the prophets and the messengers.

CHAPTER 3

LOVE FOR THE QURAN

Abdullah ibn Mas'ud [may Allah be pleased with him] said, "One day, the Prophet said to me, 'O Ibn Mas'ud, recite for me from the Quran.' I asked him, 'O Messenger of Allah, am I to read to you the Quran while the Quran was in fact revealed to you?' He said, 'I crave in listening to the recitation of the Quran from other than myself.'

Then I began reciting surah An-Nisaa. When I reach verse 41, 'So how (will it be) when We bring from every nation a witness and we bring you (O Muhammad) against these (people) as a witness?' the Prophet said to me with a loud voice, 'Enough for now.' So I raised my head to look at him and I saw in his face that the tears were flowing from his eyes."

This hadith was recorded by Imam AlBukhari, Imam Muslim, Imam Ahmad, and many of the scholars of hadith. This hadith shows us the devotion and the love that the Prophet [peace and blessings be upon him] had for the Quran wherein he would use words such as "I crave (arabic: *ashtahi*)", "I delight", "I seek", "I want" to listen to it, not just to read it from other than myself. In this hadith, there is a sense of being of the Prophet [peace and blessings be upon him] that the Quran to him was not just something put upon him as a task. The risalah of Islam was not just a burden upon Rasulullah [peace and blessings be upon him] that he had to carry and was a job that he had to fulfil.

"Ta, ha. We have not sent down to you the Quran that you be distressed. But only as a reminder for those who fear (Allah)." Surah Ta-Ha, verses 1-3.

The Prophet [peace and blessings be upon him] is the first in this example. Let's begin to study this hadith word-for-word, sentence-by-sentence to see its importance and gravity. All of us agree that the Quran is the most important link between Allah and us. In different ahadith – some of them weak, some of them hasan – the Quran being referred to as *hablullah* (the rope of Allah).

The hadith of Ali – although not a complete authentic hadith – mentioned that the Quran is referred to *hablullahi mateen*. In places surah Ali Imran, Allah Subhanallah wa Ta'ala says, "And hold firmly to the rope of Allah all together and do not become divided; and remember the favour of Allah upon you – when you are enemies and He brought your hearts together and you became, by His favour, brothers; and you were on the edge of a pit of the Fire, and He saved you from it; thus does Allah make clear to you His verses that you may be guided."

The implication of the rope of Allah is the Quran. The most significant that we hold on to as Muslims in our day to day life is the Quran. Therefore it is the most used form of ibadah. There is no ibadah that a person performs more in his day to day life than the utterance of the Quran.

Think of the prayer that we perform everyday. The Prophet [peace and blessings be upon him] says, "Prayer without reading surah Al-Fatihah is unaccepted." The basis of our prayers is the recitation of the Quran. The basis of our dua is the recitation of the Quran.

Abdullah ibn Abbas said that the most often remembered dua of the Prophet – and of us as Muslim if you were to count your dua – is "Our Lord, give us in this world (that which is) good and in the Hereafter (that which is) good and protect us from the punishment of the Fire" from surah Al-Baqarah, verse 201.

The dua that the Prophet made, "O my Lord, forgive me and my parents ..." is taken from the Quran. "... Exalted are You, indeed I have been of the wrongdoers" is taken from surah Al-Anbiya, verse 87. Also, taken from the Quran, from surah Al-Baqarah verse 255, "Allah, there is no deity except Him, the Ever-Living, the Sustainer of (all) existence ..."

The most times of worship of a believer is the recitation of the Quran.

Who is Abdullah ibn Mas'ud? He is one of the people that the Prophet [peace and blessings be upon him] said, "If you are going to learn the Quran as being something that I have taught, learn it from four people." This hadith was recorded by Imam AlBukhari.

Who do you think he began by naming? Abdullah ibn Mas'ud [may Allah be pleased with him]. According to the consensus of the sahabah, Abdullah ibn Mas'ud and Abdullah ibn Abbas are the most knowledgeable of the words of Allah, after Prophet Muhammad [peace and blessings be upon him]. Abdullah ibn Mas'ud once said, "By Allah! I have full knowledge of where every verse was revealed, to whom it was in context of, and who heard it from Prophet Muhammad."

This companion is no small individual. In fact, that is a pun. Abdullah ibn Mas'ud was a man with a very small size. Today, in our normal terms, we would describe him as a dwarf. He was someone who is very short, very small, and very skinny. In Sahih AlBukhari it is mentioned that one day, a quick moving wind came and pushed Abdullah ibn Mas'ud up into a tree. This caused his legs to get uncovered. When other companions saw his legs, they began to laugh. "Look how skinny his legs are!" The Prophet [peace and blessings be upon him] responded, "Are you amused at the thinness of his legs? By Allah! On the Day of Judgement, these legs each of them shall be the size of Uhud."

Take no assumption of this small size man. He was the one who killed Abu Lahab. In the Battle of Badr, with his own sword, he fell on Abu Lahab then ending the life of the greatest of those who opposed Prophet Muhammad [peace and blessings be upon him]. In Sahih AlBukhari, it is mentioned how Abdullah ibn Mas'ud stood in front of Abu Lahab and the bad man laughed and said to Abdullah ibn Mas'ud, "It would not be a man of your size who would end my life." After Abu Lahab got killed, Abdullah ibn Mas'ud brought his sword with the blood of Abu Lahab to the Prophet.

This was not a normal man, neither in size nor in his deeds. Prophet Muhammad [peace and blessings be upon him] is the one who teaches others and now he is asking his student, Abdullah ibn Mas'ud to recite from the Quran to him. This immediately would force the student to feel a sense of fear. Hidden gem in this hadith is the part where Abdullah ibn Mas'ud said, "When he told me to stop, I raised my head to look at him." Out of shyness and humbleness of the Messenger of Allah, Abdullah ibn Mas'ud could not look towards the Prophet while reciting the Quran.

Abdullah ibn Mas'ud said, "I recite to you when it was revealed to you, o Messenger of Allah." We learn a pivotal lesson here. The one who is a teacher, father, mother, imam, whoever it may be, is to have no shame in acquiring and learning from that who is normally seen as lesser than them. The one who is given then giving it off to others is allowed to learn from those who are less than them in size and knowledge.

Why is it that the Prophet [peace and blessings be upon him] wish to hear the Quran from other than him? Could you imagine being Rasulullah where each and every day he is the one who is instructing people in the Quran, and now in this hadith he is the one asking from Abdullah ibn Mas'ud to show him what has Abdullah learned and how he has acquired the knowledge from Rasulullah.

It is a test to Abdullah ibn Mas'ud as a way of proving to himself [peace and blessings be upon him] that he is fulfilling his obligations toward Allah. It is also a way of encouraging Abdullah ibn Mas'ud and giving him a certification. Can someone now come to Abdullah ibn Mas'ud and says, "Who are you to teach us the Quran?" when he is one of the people Prophet Muhammad [peace and blessings be upon him] listened to the Quran from?

The Prophet [peace and blessings be upon him] had listened to the Quran recitation by all four people he mentioned, such as Ubay ibn Ka'ab. Reported in Sahih AlBukhari, one day, the Prophet was walking by the house of Ubay ibn Ka'ab, he lent an ear to Ubay because he could hear Ubay reading the Quran from inside of his home. The Prophet stopped, stood outside the home of Ubay ibn Ka'ab, not speaking to anyone, and just listening to the recitation.

The next morning when the Prophet saw Ubay ibn Ka'ab, he said, "If you would have seen me yesterday, standing outside your home and listening to your recitation of the Quran, subhanallah."

As a way of encouragement and certification of these select companions, he listened to Abdullah ibn Mas'ud. However, there is an important context. Abdullah ibn Mas'ud did not take it as a matter of arrogance and a matter of conceitedness. He did not immediately began reciting the Quran to the Prophet, rather he first asked permission in a subtle way.

He said, "O Messenger of Allah, am I to read to you when it was revealed to you?" In other words, it means it is not my place to transgress this bound. Then the Prophet replied, "I crave to hear this Quran being recited from other than me."

We need to pause with this sentence. Rasulullah [peace and blessings be upon him] says, "I crave to listen to the Quran being read by other than myself." Honestly, this desire is within the Prophet while he is the one who the Quran revealed to. How much of a desire do we have in not just listening, but seeking to understand? The Quran is not like a background music, it is not something that we just hear to relax; but in it contains message.

The Prophet [peace and blessings be upon him] wished to hear from the Quran so that it would be something that he is reminded of in his life. Allah Subhanahu wa Ta'ala mentions to us, "So when the Quran is recited, then listen to it and pay attention that you may receive mercy. And remember your Lord within yourself in humility and in fear without being apparent in speech, in the mornings and the evenings, and do not be among the heedless." Surah Al-A'raf, verses 204-205.

The scholars of tafseer said this verse is in reference to those who are in the state of prayer. But its rulings is general. Thus it is also applicable that the Quran has a sense of reverence. We must be in awe with the words of Allah Subhanahu wa Ta'ala.

Hudhayfa AlYaman had a copy of the Quran. After he finished reading the Quran, he would put the Quran upon his face and he would begin to weep. Then he would say, "These are the words of my Lord."

"So how (will it be) when We bring from every nation a witness and we bring you (O Muhammad) against these (people) as a witness?" Surah An-Nisaa, verse 41.

This sense of understanding is a very important understanding for the Muslim. The Quran now has lessen in its gravity in many of the lives of the believers. The Quran now does not have the same central role that it used to have. It was inconceivable up until very lately that a Muslim household, that their children would not become fluent in the recitation of the Quran. It was inconceivable that one child would not finish the reading of the Quran with a practised qari and shaykh. For example, in Somalia. Less than twenty years ago, if an individual's children did not memorize the Quran before the age of puberty, that family was seen as a disgrace to the rest of the tribe. Subhanallah.

That was the importance that was put for the Quran. Just its utterance. Just its recitation. The first thing that was taught was always the Quran – the

Fatihah, surah Al-Ikhlas. But today in the age that we are living, in the times and in the locality that we find ourselves in, the Quran does not play a central role. Even at the time of the Prophet [peace and blessings be upon him], he complained to Allah.

"And the Messenger has said, 'O my Lord, indeed my people have taken this Quran as (a thing) abandoned.'" Surah Al-Furqan, verse 30.

The abandonment of the Quran is now a common trait in the homes of the Muslims. The scholars of hadith and the scholars of tafseer have shown us that the most important wisdom of there being such a vast amount of reward for just reading the Quran and memorizing it was as a source of protection for the letters and wording of the Quran.

Why else Allah Subhanahu wa Ta'ala makes it ten hasanat for one letter? "Bismillahirrahmanirrahim" has more than a hundred hasanat. "Alhamdulillahi rabbil 'alamin" has more than a hundred hasanat. It was a way of protecting the sanctity, the love, the usage, the syntax, the wording of the words of Allah.

"How can I read to you when it was revealed to you?" It is a way the Prophet is saying to Abdullah ibn Mas'ud, "This Quran does not just belong to me, o Abdullah ibn Mas'ud. This Quran belongs to the ummah. Everyone is to recite the Quran and everyone is to have the Quran recited to him."

Therefore, Abdullah ibn Mas'ud said, "I began to read surah An-Nisaa from its beginning." When he reached verse 41, the Prophet [peace and blessings be upon him] stopped him. He looked up and he saw the Prophet weeping due to the affect that a single verse had upon him.

The verse was, "So how (will it be) when We bring from every nation a witness and we bring you (O Muhammad) against these (people) as a witness?" This moved the Prophet [peace and blessings be upon him], cause him to well up with tears to the point that Abdullah ibn Mas'ud says, "His tears were flowing." Not that there was one tear or two tears. But his tears were flowing.

"Has the time not come for those who have believed that their hearts should become humbly submissive at the remembrance of Allah and what has come down of the truth? And let them not be like those who were given the Scripture before, and a long period passed over them, so their hearts hardened; and many of them are defiantly disobedient." Surah Al-Hadid, verse 16.

In surah Az-Zumar, verse 23, Allah describes the Quran. "Allah has sent down the best statement: a consistent Book wherein is reiteration; the skin shiver therefrom of those who fear their Lord; then their skin and their hearts relax at the remembrance of Allah; that is the guidance of Allah by which He guides whom He wills, and one whom Allah leaves astray, for him there is no guide."

Those who have true faith will have goosebumps when they hear the recitation of the Quran. The Quran has a very significant role in the life of the Muslim in the manners that we put upon our soul, in the training and education of our inner self. There are numerous examples for this from the life of others, not just of the Prophet [peace and blessings be upon him]. This is not just the trait of Rasulullah.

Let's look at some of the stories of some of the companions. For example, Urwah ibn AzZubair [may Allah be pleased with him]. He mentions that A'isha [may Allah be pleased with her] was his maternal aunt. It means that he could come into her house, he could see her daily activities within her home. He had access to her that others did not have.

Urwah ibn AzZubair said, "One day, I came in and I said assalamualaikum, but I noticed that she was praying and I noticed that she was standing in tasbih." It is another word for standing in prayer. "And she was reading just this one verse while she was praying, 'So Allah conferred favour upon us and protected us from the punishment of the scorching Fire.'" (Surah At-Tur, verse 27)

A'isha [may Allah be pleased with her] would recite it and paused and began to make dua to Allah Subhanahu wa Ta'ala while weeping. She would repeat this verse over and over again, while standing in prayer. Nothing else.

Urwah ibn AzZubair said, "So I stood behind her, waiting for her to finish her prayer until I became tired. So, I went to the market to buy some of the essentials that I have needed. When I came back from the market, she was still there in standing position, reciting the same verse as if nothing have changed."

Another example is of Umar ibn AlKhattab [may Allah be pleased with him]. While he was Amirul Mukminin, he stood up leading the people in prayer, and he was reciting to them surah Yusuf. Then he began to weep until his chest and clothing was drenched from his weeping.

There is also example of Abu Bakar AsSiddiq [may Allah be pleased with him]. During his time as the Khalifa, people from Yemen came to meet him. Then they asked him, "Recite for us something from the Quran." When they heard him reciting the Quran, they wept out of fear of Allah Subhanahu wa Ta'ala.

Then they say, "O Abu Bakar, we used to be like these people until our heart hardened." The hardening of the heart is the most significant reason that a person is distracted from the words of Allah.

Therefore, it is important for us to take account of ourselves, to see from this example of Prophet Muhammad [peace and blessings be upon him] that the Quran is to play a central role in our life.

What are the important lessons that we are to extract from this hadith and from this verse that was recited by Abdullah ibn Mas'ud to the Prophet.

First, to display the Quran, to read the Quran for someone, to ask someone to read for you, or for you to ask someone to listen to you reading the Quran is part of the sunnah of the Prophet. It is the most important attribute of the believer that he wishes to listen to the Quran, that he wants to enjoy the recitation of the Quran, that someone corrects him in his pronunciation or in his understanding of the Quran. It is important for us to have this desire because it is from the sunnah of Prophet Muhammad [peace and blessings be upon him].

Second, the one who is beneficial to others should never be conceited or arrogant to think that he cannot benefit from those whom he has taught. The best of teachers is the one who is continually learning. You cannot become a good teacher and you cannot have enough knowledge unless you are continually learning. This is found in many of the different disciplines in Islam and in Islamic law. For example, Imam AshShafie – a young man age 10 or 11 – correcting Imam Malik in the Prophet's mosque. Imam Malik was his teacher, superior, and his leader. Meanwhile, scholars are also seen correcting and revising one another. Knowing that one of them is more knowledgeable was never a deterrent from speaking the word of truth if one was sure it is the truth. Never feel that as a person who is not seemingly as knowledgeable as the teacher or the imam that you do not have a right to question or to benefit others. Instruct others with the truth even if it is a single verse.

Third, from the principle of fiqh that we see is that if you are a person listening, you have a right to say to the one reading, "Please, could you stop for a moment." You have the right to leave because there is no sign of disrespect to the Quran or to the reader if you say "Jazakallahu khayran" and stand and leave. Or if you are listening to a tape and you pause it to do something else. There is no harm in listening to the Quran when your attention is with it. But there is harm in being distracted from what is being recited. It is either you are with it or you stop and do something else. However, this does not negate the fact that an individual has the right to listen while doing other things. You might be a shop owner and you are listening to the Quran while doing your tasks.

Fourth, reading the Quran in an event is a sunnah that is established from the life of the Prophet [peace and blessings be upon him]. Any time a group or brothers or a group of sisters gather, it is a sunnah for them that they will either begin or conclude or mention verses from the Quran in their discussion. It does not matter what the discussions are all about. Someone is visiting your home, someone is leaving your home, after a meal, before a meal; any time there is a gathering of people, it is a sunnah that there is even just a single verse as a reminder of Allah Subhanahu wa Ta'ala. That is from the established characteristics of people of piety.

Fifth, contemplating and reflecting upon what is being recited. It is worthless for an individual just to sit as a parrot without wishing to know more about what he is reading. This does not solely mean for the one who does not understand Arabic. In fact, many people who can speak, read, and write Arabic feel lost when they are reading the Quran Arabic. It means that the one who reads the Quran in whatever language that he originally is from, he must have a desire to want to learn its meaning, to learn its interpretation, to learn its context, and to learn its rulings. There must be more than just physical utterance of the Quran.

Therefore, there is a select rewards for those who are proficient in the reading and in the understanding of the Quran, in comparison to those who just recite the Quran. It is more important to read with wisdom, understanding, and clarity of what is being recited than it is just to recite without understanding or meaning.

Umm Salamah described the recitation by the Prophet [peace and blessings be upon him] by saying, "He would recite the Quran by stopping at the end of each verse, or at the end of each area where the meaning is most profound, as a way of emphasizing the meanings, as a way of showing the importance of this particular section. He would repeat the same verse over and over again as a way of emphasizing the particular sections that he wish for the people to understand."

We learn now that the recitation of the Quran moved Prophet Muhammad [peace and blessings be upon him] to tears, even when he himself was not the reciter. This is a significant fact for us.

Many of us are not proficient in the readings of the Quran. However, we all have the capability to listen to the Quran. The scholars such as Imam AnNawawi and Imam AdhDhahabi had stated that the one who is unable to read the Quran with proficiency, but sits with individuals who read the Quran, or listens to the Quran being recited, seeking the same reward as the reader is given equal reward.

If you are unable to read the Quran with perfect tajweed, but you sit and studying it with an individual who is fluent in his recitation, the reward of his recitation is given to you as well for listening and being cognitive. The rewards are not just limited to reciting, but there are also equal to the one who is in full attention of the recitation of the Quran.

CHAPTER 4

PRAYER

When Prophet Muhammad [peace and blessings be upon him] would come to pray, it is as if there was a sound of water boiling in a copper kettle within his chest. It means his weeping in the recitation of the Quran could be audibly heard as he was leading the people in salah. This authentic hadith was reported by Imam Ahmad, Ibn AlMubarak, and Abu Daud.

Let's pause to see the significance of this hadith. First, the sahabah took note of everything. Nothing from the mannerisms of the Prophet [peace and blessings be upon him] was left untouched. They even take account of the sound that his chest made and his wheezing in his recitation. They would say, "On this day, when the Prophet was reading the surah, I could hear his chest wheezing from the sound of his crying in his prayer."

As reported in Sahih AlBukhari, when the Prophet [peace and blessings be upon him] was leading the people in Asr prayer – the prayer when the recitation is not loud – one of the sahabah said, "The Prophet read in it surah Al-Mursalat." He was asked, "How do you know?" He replied, "I could see his beard moving and I recognized from the movement of his lips and his beard that that was surah Al-Mursalat." That was how observant they were of Rasulullah [peace and blessings be upon him].

This is the first and most important lesson. Muhammad [peace and blessings be upon him] to them was the sanctual part of their life. His physical being as well. In an authentic hadith reported by Imam AlBukhari, one of the companions came to the Prophet [peace and blessings be upon him] weeping. The Prophet asked him, "Why are you crying?" The man said, "O Rasulullah, when you are living now with us, when I crave to see you, I come and I can see you and I am led in prayer by you. Then I thought of the day that I would leave the worldly life and I would not have the opportunity to be led in prayer by you, or to come to the mosque and see you when I want; so I began to cry and I came back from my home to sit with you once again."

The man then continued, "If in the dunya I was privileged enough to be with Muhammad [peace and blessings be upon him], surely in the akhirah, o Rasulullah, you will be in the highest places in Jannah, and as well as I will do, I will never reach the level that you will reach. So I fear that once this worldly life ends, I will never get to sit and be in your company."

The Prophet [peace and blessings be upon him] replied, "You will be with the one you love."

This is a very significant hadith. You will be with the one you love. How much love and desire do we have for Rasulullah [peace and blessings be upon him]? How much want and need do we have that is displayed in positive actions in our lives. Pivotal moments in our lives that bring about constructive change. From the hadith, the companion weeping and returning back from home fearing that in Jannah – if he was to make it there – he will not be in the company of Rasulullah [peace and blessings be upon him].

Muhammad [peace and blessings be upon him] held a permanent, positive, important role in all of their lives. The above hadith gives us great hope. In the hadith mentioned the people who lived with the Prophet. But now let's think about us who have not seen him.

As reported in an authentic hadith, one day the Prophet said to the sahabah, "They are my beloved." The sahabah asked, "Who is it that you love? The Muhajirin or the Ansar?" Rasulullah replied, "Not those ones. The one that I have love for are those who believe in me and have never seen me."

It is important for us to look at how the companions paid attention to Rasulullah [peace and blessings be upon him] and how observant they were of him. Try to implement that in our lives.

In leading the people in prayer, the Prophet [peace and blessings be upon him] wished to emphasize for them certain verses and to show them the rewards they would receive and remind them of the punishment that would be implemented for those who have sinned. One of the most powerful tools of the Prophet's usage was his ability to stir the hearts.

In Sahih Muslim, the companions described the Prophet [peace and blessings be upon him] when he was given a khutbah. They said his eyes would become red and he would command them of an enemy that was coming to attack. Through this, we learn that the Prophet's subtle influence to the companions was as simple as being humbling himself to Allah. His weeping was not for show for the sahabah or to move them. Instead, it is out of his fear of Allah.

If Muhammad [peace and blessings be upon him] the one whom Allah has declared in the Quran, "You were the one whom Allah has forgiven on what has happened, then what would happen."

"Indeed, We have given you, (O Muhammad), a clear conquest. That Allah may forgive for you what preceded of your sin and what will follow and complete his favour upon you and guide you to a straight path. And (that) Allah may aid you with a mighty victory." Surah Al-Fath, verses 1-3.

If he is moved out of his love, out of his fear, and out of his hope and desire for Allah's mercy to be in that state, where are we from it?

First lesson we extract from this hadith is that if one is reciting the Quran in prayer and due to the weeping or due to him reciting the Quran with a sense of weeping that changes his voice, and some of the rules of tajweed are missed, the prayer is still valid.

Second lesson, the most complete of individuals who was mindful and fearing of Allah Subhanahu wa Ta'ala was the Prophet [peace and blessings be upon him]. None attain the greatest sense of fear and love and hope for his Creator more than the Master of

Humanity, Muhammad [peace and blessings be upon him].

Third lesson, when a person recites the Quran and weeps in his prayer, it is a good sign of his humbleness to Allah, if his weeping is for Allah and for none other. We are not seeking to please or show off to anyone of our deeds. It is solely for the pleasure of Allah Subhanahu wa Ta'ala.

Fourth lesson, there is to be no exaggeration. At times, you will find there are people who exaggerate what is not found in their recitation of the Quran. They will go to bounce and out of bounce with their raising of voice or weeping. We do not hear this from the sunnah of the Prophet [peace and blessings be upon him]. The most that is reported from him is that he simply wept as if his chest had the sound of kettle boiling water. There was no wailing, no screaming, no loud audible sounds or screeching; it was simple fear towards Allah. The exaggerated actions is in fact contrary to the sunnah of the Prophet [peace and blessings be upon him].

CHAPTER 5

SIGNS FROM ALLAH

Abdullah ibn Amr ibn Al'As [may Allah be pleased with them] narrated, "The sun during the life of the Prophet [peace and blessings be upon him] was eclipsed by the moon." Reported by Imam AlBukhari, Imam Muslim, and many other scholars.

It means that either the whole of the sun or part of it was eclipsed so that its light was not seen in the way that is normally appreciated everyday. When this natural phenomena happened, the Prophet [peace and blessings be upon him] hurried to the mosque and began to lead the people in prayer. He recited from the Quran until the companions who were praying behind him thought that he would continue reading and he would not make ruku'. That was how long the Prophet recited in the prayer.

In other narration of this hadith, some of the companions said the Prophet [peace and blessings be upon him] read Al-Baqarah and Ali Imran in the first rakaah. Then abruptly he went into ruku'. He bowed towards Allah Subhanahu wa Ta'ala for such an extended period that the people behind him thought he was not going to rise up from it. He then straighten from the ruku' and people thought he would not go into sujood. When he performed the sujood, it was as if he was not going to rise up from it. He then sat between the two sajdah until the companions thought he was not going to make another sujood from the length that each of these time periods entailed. He then made another sujood and continued with another rakaah of similar length.

In his prayer, it was described as he would have a heavy breathing in his recitation of the Quran and he was excessive in his weeping. His dua throughout the prayer, "My Lord, have You not promised that You would not send us punishment while I am amongst the sahabah? And I am here with them, making dua to You. Have You not promised that You would not punish them while they are seeking Your forgiveness? And here I am and all of us are seeking Your forgiveness."

"But Allah would not punish them while you, (O Muhammad) are among them, and Allah would not would not punish them while they seek forgiveness." Surah Al-Anfal, verse 33.

The Prophet continued with the prayer in this form. Shortly after he had concluded his prayer, the sun began to re-emerge from behind the eclipse. Then he stood up, he praised Allah, and sought nearness to Allah Subhanahu wa Ta'ala, and said to the companions, "Surely the sun and the moon are two of Allah's distinct signs. They are created by Allah and Allah will use them at different times as a sign to mankind of different things. They do not eclipse one another due to the death of any individual and not to the birth of any individual. If there is another eclipse, then run hurriedly and in fear to the remembrance of Allah."

This hadith is the narration of Abdullah ibn Amr ibn Al'As [may Allah be pleased with them]. In this hadith are many different subjects that intertwined. Some of the questions that may arise in hearing this hadith are events that we assume that will happen in the sun and the moon, or are these the things that we are to be afraid of, or isn't this something that is ancient, or isn't this something that is natural phenomena, and so on and so forth.

Also, why is it that the Prophet [peace and blessings be upon him] mentioned with precision that there is no life or death over an individual that is to be associated with these signs? Next, you might want to ask why is the sun and the moon a sign from Allah Subhanahu wa Ta'ala? How are they signs from Allah? The other question is what was the Prophet afraid of? Why did he order us to come to the mosque and pray if there is an eclipse? What are there to fear? This is something that happens millions of miles away from us. What is the point of fear in this issue?

All of these are valid questions why was the Prophet [peace and blessings be upon him] weeping. We find the secret to many of these by studying the context of the hadith. It would surprise you to know that on this very same day, the Prophet's son, Ibrahim passed away. When he carried his son and wept, he said, "The eyes shed tears and the heart felt sorrow. By your departure, o Ibrahim, we feel sadness and sorrow."

On that same day, this incident of the sun being eclipsed by the moon occurred. At that moment, the companions said that it is due to the death of the Prophet's son.

Prophet Muhammad [peace and blessings be upon him] was a person of integrity. If he was not a person of truthful, he would have simply said, "Yes, it is true. I am the Prophet of Allah and because of my sadness, the sun and the moon perform this miraculous occurrence for you to believe in my truthful."

Instead we see him said something completely opposite. The complete opposite of what a normal prophet and messenger would say. He did not seek to prove his prophethood to anyone using something that was not given to him by Allah Subhanahu wa Ta'ala. This is a very pivotal moment in the life of Prophet Muhammad [peace and blessings be upon him], in the integrity of his message that he does not need any other evidence or a miraculous sign. He just wish to explain to the companions the reality of the affairs, the truth of the matter in all issues and in all circumstances.

It has been said that the Prophet [peace and blessings be upon him] ran to the mosque and he prayed because in the Quran, Allah Subhanahu wa Ta'ala says, "So when vision is dazzled. And the moon darkens. And the sun and the moon are joined." This is a sign that Allah has stated in the Quran literally as being a sign of the coming of times, of a change to happen. Not for the life or death of an individual, not for the birth of an individual; but it is a sign for humanity that there is more out there in the world than what you appreciate. There are things beyond your control. Thus, this is a sign that is direct from the Quran.

"... and We send not the signs except as a warning." Surah Al-Isra, verse 59.

Do not think that these natural phenomena that occur are things that now due to the understanding that we have of how they occur and that they now limit the influence they should have upon ourselves and our hearts. Think of the magnitude and the precision of the creation of Allah Subhanahu wa Ta'ala when he causes certain things to happen to produce a fact that witness hundreds of thousands, in fact, millions of miles away. We have to think a little bit bigger than what is in and around us.

According to scientists, there is not only one universe. But instead, there are many universes or multiverse. Physicists are saying that the farthest of universes from what we experience is more than a trillion light years away. That is a phenomenal number. That is a number that you cannot compute and understand. To make it a little bit clear, it would be like a grain of sand in our solar system. A grain of sand is the size of the earth in comparison to what we have observed of our singular universe.

It is a concept that is difficult to perceive and to rationalize. It is something that can only be demonstrated theoretically in numbers. There is no projections that can show it to you.

Allah Subhanahu wa Ta'ala has created a vast expanse. He created the heavens and the earth. The light of the stars that we see today is not an instantaneous projections. Instead, the light has been travelling to you for millions of light years. Thus, what you are seeing today is in fact millions of light years old. What is there now is different than what you are seeing. Subhanallah.

"Then I swear by the setting of the stars. And indeed, it is an oath – if you could know – (most) great. Indeed, it is a noble Quran. In a Register well-protected." Surah Al-Waqi'ah, verses 75-78.

Allah Subhanahu wa Ta'ala give us as an oath the

distance and the locations of the stars. If you actually understood the weight of this oath of Allah, it is something great. You actually appreciated it.

Allah Subhanahu wa Ta'ala mentions to us numerous details. He begins surah An-Nahl by saying, "The command of Allah is coming, so be not impatient for it; exalted is He and high above what they associate with Him. He sends down the angels, with the inspiration of His command, upon whom He wills of His servants, (telling them), 'Warn that there is no deity except Me; so fear Me.'"

The Day of Judgement has already come, but do not wait for it to happen. It means that the order of the Day of Judgement has already been given. Because it is such a long distance of travel, this order is coming to us but yet to arrive.

Do not be of those whose heart has become closed to the verses of Allah. He mentions to us many magnificent things in the Quran. We will leave even the traditions of the Prophet [peace and blessings be upon him] and just focus on the words of Allah.

"Do you not see that to Allah prostrates whoever is in the heavens and whoever is on the earth and the sun, the moon, the stars, the mountains, the trees, the moving creatures and many of the people? But upon many the punishment has been justified; and he whom Allah humiliates, for him there is no bestower of honor; indeed, Allah does what he wills." Surah Al-Hajj, verse 18.

There is more than what we can perceive, understand, and rationalize. The physical dimensions of the world that we appreciate are set in rules and laws by Allah and The One who sets them is The One who able to expand them, to contract them, or to suspend them. He is The One who is able.

Prophet Muhammad [peace and blessings be upon him] is the one who has gone on an Isra and Mi'raj, raised to the heaven, have seen the Jannah and the Fire, has gone through the seven levels of heaven. When we appreciate this fact, we will appreciate and understand the sign from Allah, such as the sun and the moon eclipse because the Prophet [peace and blessings be upon him] himself fearful of this phenomena and he wept.

Do not feel arrogant just because you have seen the eclipse on television and just because you understand about the synchronicity of the orbits. There is more to the signs of Allah. When He shows them to us, we appreciate it. There is more to the apparent natural physical environments and the world that have been created around us than we can appreciate.

What are the lessons that we can learn from this hadith?

First, the Prophet [peace and blessings be upon him] is fearful of Allah, although he is assured by Allah. The Prophet has been confirmed by Allah that he will not be punished and the companions will not be punished as long as he remain with them and as long as they are making istighfar. Therefore, he pleaded to Allah. He taught us that the heart shift and thus he would make a dua, "O Allah who can cause the heart to shift from righteousness to lack-off, make our heart steady and firm upon your faith."

Even the Prophet [peace and blessings be upon him] was fearful for himself and the companions. When he would see signs, he would be fearful towards Allah.

Second, the Prophet [peace and blessings be upon him] put to rest one of the ignorant beliefs of the pre-

Islamic Arabs. It is that when someone famous or someone important was giving birth or the death of an individual, the sun or the moon would be eclipse. Even when it was something that he could use as a proof of his sanctity and his prophethood, he rejected it. Because it is from the pagan's tradition. Rather, we believe the sun and the moon do not have any influence on the life or death of an individual.

Third, the Prophet [peace and blessings be upon him] was always fearful of his ummah. When he is in prayer, he does not say, "O Allah, do not punish me, do not send disgrace upon me …." He says, "O Allah, You have promised that my ummah will not be harmed while they are making istighfar and I am with them." Subhanallah. That was the tenderness, the love of Rasulullah [peace and blessings be upon him] for his ummah.

Fourth, it is important for the Muslims at the times of eclipse or natural phenomena that their first instinct is to come towards Allah. It is to be reminded of Allah, to look up to the sky and say, "Subhanallah, this is a sign from Allah." Not that it is a sign of destruction or not that it is something that will bring about turmoil. When Prophet Muhammad [peace and blessings be upon him] was in Madinah and suddenly the swift wind came, he would go to the mosque. He would turn to the remembrance of Allah. That has always been the trait of the believers. We are always returning to Allah Subhanahu wa Ta'ala when anything out of the ordinary strikes us.

Nothing saves any individual from any harm or any near harm that is greater than dua and prayer.

CHAPTER 6

DEATH OF HIS GRANDSON

Iman AlBukhari and Imam Muslim recorded: Usama ibn Zayd [may Allah be pleased with him] said, "We were in the company of Prophet Muhammad [peace and blessings be upon him] when one of his daughters sent a messenger to hurriedly bring him. She sent a young boy to come and say, 'O Rasulullah, please come. My son, your grandson is in the state of near death.' The Prophet said to the messenger, 'Return to her and tell her that I have been informed and I say to her to Allah is that which He has given you in the first place. And to Him belongs what He is taking back from you. And everything with Allah has a return record and account. Tell her to be patient and to hold this as being a source of reward for her in the next life.'

The Prophet [peace and blessings be upon him] did not get up and rushed to his daughter. He sent back the messenger with these orders. After a few minutes, the messenger came back to the Prophet [peace and blessings be upon him] and said, 'O Rasulullah, she says please, by Allah, come to me.' So the Prophet [peace and blessings be upon him] hearing her wishing for him to come and she has used an invocation for Allah. Then the Prophet stood up immediately and he took with him Sa'ad ibn Ubadah, Mu'adh ibn Jabal, and I went with them."

The young child was breathing with the labour breathing. They put him in the arm of the Prophet and he was taking very shallow, small breaths. The Prophet's eyes overflowed with tears. Sa'ad said to him, "O Rasulullah, what is this that we see?" The Prophet replied, "This tears are a mercy that Allah has put." Allah put mercy in the heart of His servants and surely Allah is Most Merciful to those whom His servants show mercy to.

There are many lessons we learn from this hadith. First, as soon as an individual is informed of a hardship, the most important thing is to remind them of Allah. The Prophet [peace and blessings be upon him] did not get up and did not rush. He was not in the state of panic. His daughter sent a messenger to tell him, "Hurry o Rasulullah, my son is dying. Your grandson is dying!" He responded to her with that which she needs to hear first. "Inform her that Muhammad [peace and blessings be upon him] says to her surely what you have been given from Allah, already belongs to Him. And what He is taking from you also His. And everything has its appointed time with Allah. Be patient and hold it as a reward with Allah Subhanahu wa Ta'ala."

This shows us that the Prophet [peace and blessings be upon him] treated everything in a measure that it deserved. Our first instinct is to rush over and ask, "How can I help? What can we do?" But here we see the Prophet was giving the spiritual grounding that which is most needed. Regardless of the outcome, whatever you have is already from Allah. If he was to take it back, it is from Allah Subhanahu wa Ta'ala. And everything has an appointed time.

Second, the Prophet [peace and blessings be upon him] asked other people to come with him. Usually in Islam and from the teaching of sunnah of the Prophet, only those who are invited are allowed to show up. We do not crash a party. If a brother has a waleema and I am invited, I do not come after praying Maghrib and say, "Come with me, there is a waleema." In the joyful moments of the Muslims' life, we do not attend, except with invitation. Therefore we see from the right of a Muslim on a Muslim, if he invites you, you must answer. But then if he becomes ill, even if he does not invite, it is your right to go and visit him. There is a huge difference.

From the hadith, the Prophet [peace and blessings be upon him] took with him the three companions to visit the young child and his daughter.

Third, you are to make your best effort to fulfil the oath of another Muslim. If a Muslim says to you "Wallahi, do this" or "By Allah, I ask you for this", you are to do the best of your ability to fulfil and to make ibrar for the oath. His daughter said, "I ask you by Allah, to do this particular deed", so immediately without question, the Prophet [peace and blessings be upon him] stood up and went to answer her call.

Fourth, it is more important to begin with greeting even in time of difficulty than to begin immediately with the words that you need to say. His daughter sent this messenger and she told the boy to send salam to the Prophet and inform him that his grandchild is suffering illness.

Fifth, it is a duty upon the imams, the elders, the people of barakah, the people who have been consistent in their deeds of Islam that they should be the first to visit the ill. It is more of an obligation for them than for the younger. This is from the sunnah of the Prophet [peace and blessings be upon him].

Sixth, the invitation of the daughter of the Prophet carried the title of Rasulullah [peace and blessings be upon him]. She did not say to the messenger, "Go tell my father ..." She said, "Go inform Rasulullah ..." It shows for every individual who has deserved an honoured position that that honoured position is the sacred part of their personality and the importance of their character. Everyone is to accommodate with that. This is part of the tradition in Islam.

Seventh, weeping and shedding tears at difficult times is not a sign of weakness. Sa'ad said to Prophet Muhammad [peace and blessings be upon him], "What is this tears?" Sa'ad is an Arab man and from the people who grew up in the harsh desert climate. It is recorded in Sahih AlBukhari that one day, the Prophet was walking by and his grandson AlHasan or AlHussain came and the Prophet kissed him on his cheek. One of the Bedouins who has entered into Islam saw the Prophet kissing his young grandson. The Bedouin said, "What is this? I have ten children. I have never kissed any single one of them." The Prophet [peace and blessings be upon him] said, "What am I to do with a man who has no mercy in his heart?"

The heart needs to have love and mercy to the young children. A man asked Ali [may Allah be pleased with him], "Who of your children do you love the most?" Obviously he has AlHasan and AlHussain – the greatest of the grandchildren of Prophet Muhammad, the most beloved of the youth to the Prophet. They would come and sit on his shoulders as he prayed. They would sit on his back in his sujood. He would carry them on the mimbar as he was giving his Friday and Eid sermons. They were beloved by the Prophet.

"O Ali, who of your children do you love the most?" Ali said, "The young one until he is old. And the one who is ill until he feels better. And the one who is travelling from me until he returns to me." That is the mercy that is found in the heart of the sahabah.

One day, after the death of the Prophet [peace and blessings be upon him] and during the khilafah of Ali [may Allah be pleased with him], one of the companions' sons went out in battle defending Islam. Soon after, the companion heard news of their shahadah. They had been martyred. Ali had not yet been informed about this news. When he came, he saw the face of this companion looked like someone is feeling sorrow in his heart. Ali then asked, "Why do I see you depressed and sorrow?" The companion replied, "All of my sons have been martyred today." Subhanallah. Not one nor two. But all of his sons have been martyred.

Ali [may Allah be pleased with him] said to him, "The one who is pleased by the destiny of Allah upon him, the destiny of Allah will happens whether he likes it or not. And he will received the reward for being pleased with what Allah Subhanahu wa Ta'ala has decided. The one who is not pleased by what Allah has ordered upon him, what he is not pleased with will still happen and he will not receive the reward. Therefore, it is better to have a sense of honour even at the times of sorrow, a sense of hope in Allah and ask Allah to give you better than what you had."

Remember the reaction of Ummu Salamah [may Allah be pleased with her] the wife of the Prophet. She was married to Abu Salamah before she was married to Rasulullah. Abu Salamah was a distinguished husband. When Ummu Salamah heard the news of her husband's death, she said, "Who is better than Abu Salamah that will propose to me?" Abu Bakar went, she rejected him. Then Umar, Uthman, and Ali. None she thought could equate to Abu Salamah. When she heard of the Prophet [peace and blessings be upon him], she said to him, "O Rasulullah, what dua should I make?" The Prophet replied, "Say innalillahi wa inna ilaihi raji'un and ask Allah to give you someone better than him." However, she did not have anyone in her mind that eventually the Prophet [peace and blessings be upon him] would come and seek her hand. Subhanallah. There is always a positive to any attribute that we find in our lives.

Eighth, it is a sunnah to invite the people of knowledge and people of taqwa to your home to ask Allah Subhanahu wa Ta'ala to alleviate any of your harm, your ailments, or your sickness. You should not be shy to ask some of the brothers and sisters to make dua for you. You should not be shy to ask some of the brothers and sisters to visit someone of your beloved in the hospital. That is from the sunnah of Prophet Muhammad [peace and blessings be upon him.

Ninth, when a person who is in pain, there is no harm in asking for help. If a person feels that they cannot deal with a situation, they can look for assistance. There is no harm if an individual who feels they are unable to help to resist from entering into that which they are requested for. When his daughter asked for the first time, the Prophet [peace and blessings be upon him], he did not get up and go to her aide. He waited. He gave her advice to the best of his ability at that time. Then later, he went to fulfil the obligation that Allah Subhanahu wa Ta'ala had obligated him upon in answering her invocation with the dua to Allah.

DEATH OF HIS SAHABAH

This companion was one of the people who embraced Islam in the very early moments. He was one of the first 50 individuals who accepted the message that was delivered to Rasulullah [peace and blessings be upon him].

His name was Uthman ibn Madh'un. He was one of the greatest companions of the Prophet [peace and blessings be upon him] and to appreciate this moment in the life of the Prophet, it is important to give a few words regarding this great companion.

He had many issues that came to be with the Prophet [peace and blessings be upon him], many significant moments that were traced in the seerah of Rasulullah's life. This honourable man was of the few Arabs who prohibited upon himself alcohol before Islam and before the risalah was given to Muhammad [peace and blessings be upon him].

He is famous and written in the pre-Islamic poets' tongues for having said the following words: I will not consume anything that clouds my mind, removes my sanity, causes me the ability to judge what is right and what is wrong to be abandoned. And I will not consume anything that will cause people who are beneath me in size and in intelligence to mock and to laugh at me. I will not consume anything that will cause me to give my daughter or my sister or someone who is beloved to me in marriage to someone whom I normally would not accept.

Even before Islam, Uthman ibn Madh'un had these noble characteristics and was of the people who had a great deal of clarity and wisdom. He was also one of the individuals from the companions who made the two hijrah. He first migrated to Al Habasha (Ethiopia), and later to Madinah AlMunawwarah. He was from those who witness the Battle of Badr, who fought alongside the Prophet [peace and blessings be upon him] in defence of Islam, he is described by other companions as a true worshipper of Allah and a person who did not put much importance in the worldly matters. He was the first person to be buried in the Al Baqi, the cemetery of the Muslims near the Prophet's mosque.

A'isha [may Allah be pleased with her] said, "Rasulullah went to see Uthman while he had passed away. He fell upon Uthman, reached down to him, hugged him, kissed him in his face, and then began to weep greatly until I could see the tears consistently and constantly flowing down his face." This hadith was recorded by Imam Abu Daud and Imam Ahmad.

The Prophet [peace and blessings be upon him] was having a great deal of emotion for this particular companion. The commentators on this hadith reported many different reasons. First, this companion was one of the first individuals who came in support of the Prophet [peace and blessings be upon him] during his early days in Makkah. This companion was also the first people who defended Islam in Al Habasha, who went along with Jafar and others, spoke to the people of Al Habasha, calling them to Islam when they were forced out of Makkah. This companion witnessed the Battle of Badr. He defended Islam when other people did not have an opportunity to come in the defense of Rasulullah [peace and blessings be upon him].

The Prophet [peace and blessings be upon him] showed a great deal of love towards this particular companion.

In this hadith also there are fiqh matters that we can extract. First, in Islam we have a lot of reverence for the deceased. But it does not transgress the bounds of the norm. It means that as Muslims, the deceased has their rights – we cleanse him, we perform the kafan, we do the prayer. In addition to these, we also we have attachment for them. The worldly life is not seen as completely separate from the hereafter. As Muslims, it is very symbolic for us to see the deceased, to carry them upon our shoulders as it is more sunnah compared to putting them on a cart. At the time of the Prophet [peace and blessings be upon him], he would try to maximize the time that the deceased were in contact with the human being.

The Prophet [peace and blessings be upon him] came into the room, uncovered the man's face, wept near him, kissed him, hugged on to him. This was also the habit of those came after the Prophet. And this man is a significant individual, but when we compare him to the greatness of Rasulullah [peace and blessings be upon him], he is insignificant.

For a few moment, let us ponder the greatest calamity that befell the Muslim ummah in its entirety. The scholars of Islam mention that there was no tragedy that the Muslim ummah face greater than the death of Prophet Muhammad [peace and blessings be upon him]. He is the one who the companions had the greatest love for, and therefore his death, his separation from this worldly life to many other faiths, other people, other disciplines, and other studies; it would have brought an end to Islam. In fact, it was a lesson that was taught to the companions many years earlier.

In the Battle of Uhud, as recorded in the Quran, the mushrikin tried to cause a disturbance amongst the Muslim ranks. One of the mushrikin stood up during the battle and said, "We have killed Muhammad!" Lying in a disgraceful lie. Some of the companions heard this word. As recorded in Sahih AlBukhari, they threw down their weapons, their swords, their shields, their arrows, and their bows. They sat on the ground weeping, thinking that Muhammad [peace and blessings be upon him] has passed away. They did not have the mobility and the effort that they had just a moment before hearing this news – which was a lie.

One of the companions, Anas ibn Nadhr, came and seeing these companions sitting in multitude in the middle of the battlefield, throwing their weapons, no longer defending the Prophet [peace and blessings be upon him], thinking that the battle has ended and that

Islam will be vanquished. Anas said, "What happened? What are you waiting for?" They replied, "We have heard Muhammad has died." Anas said, "Stand up and give your life for what he gave his life for."

Allah immediately brought down surah Ali Imran, verse 144, the translation says, "Muhammad is not but a messenger; (other) messengers have passed on before him; so if he was to die or be killed, would you turn your back on your heels (to unbelief)? And he who turns back on his heels will never harm Allah at all; but Allah will reward the grateful."

The Prophet's life was lived to the fullest – in calling people to the tawheed of Allah. And yet, at the moment of the separation from his worldly life, we find the greatest of lessons. Similar to what we find in the story of Uthman ibn Madh'un.

A few days before the Prophet's death, he goes to the buried places of people of Uhud, people of Badr, and people of Al Baqi. He gives them his salam and he begins to weep severely. Some of the companions notice the Prophet has done this on numerous occasions. Every morning and every duha, he would go to the people who have passed away and give them his salam.

One day, upon returning, he says to A'isha, "O A'isha, I feel that I have the flu." During the pre-Islamic time, Madinah AlMunawwara is famous of being a place where it was easy to catch infectious disease that cause you to be tired, to have high temperature, and to have symptoms of illness. A'isha was also was suffering this at the time of the Prophet.

The Prophet [peace and blessings be upon him] went home and he asked Abu Bakar AsSiddiq to lead the people in prayers. For many days, the Prophet would sit in his home. Every so often, he would ask his wives to bring tumblers of cool water to bathe him in it. And he complained to Allah of his ailment. A few days before his death, he emerged – not having led the people in prayer now for more than ten days. Thirteen days before the Prophet [peace and blessings be upon him] death, he stood on the mimbar after asking Ali [may Allah be pleased with him] to carry him and he gave the ummah the greatest of advices.

He said to them, "I remind you of your prayers, your prayers. While Allah is with you, the Muhajirin, when you came into this city of Madinah, those who supported you were the Ansar. Do not neglect them and do not forget them." Then he said to the Ansar, "When the Muhajirin came, you open your homes to them and Allah blessed you for having done so."

Then the Prophet [peace and blessings be upon him] recited surah An-Nasr. "When the victory of Allah has come and the conquest, and you see the people entering into the religion of Allah in multitudes, then exalt (Him) with praise of your Lord and ask forgiveness of Him; indeed, He is ever accepting of repentance."

Immediately upon reciting the surah, Abu Bakar AsSiddiq stood up, weeping – understanding the meaning of the surah. He said, "May I be sacrificed instead of you, o Messenger of Allah! May my son be the one in your place, o Rasulullah." Because the companions do not understand the consequence of the surah, they looked to Abu Bakar as if he just said something strange. Little that they know that this was the final instructions from Allah to the Prophet [peace and blessings be upon him]. That was the last time he stood in front of his people in admonition and in discussion to them.

After being carried back to his room, his condition worsened. A'isha, who at this time was his sole caretaker, began to take care of him. Every time he would fall unconscious, he would wake up and say, "Have the people prayed?" A'isha would inform him, "They have prayed their dhuhr." And each times of prayer.

Then the Prophet would go back into unconsciousness and wake up and asked her, "O A'isha, how much money do I have left in my possession?" A'isha said, "You have nothing but seven coins left." He said, "Give them in charity, o A'isha. How will Muhammad condition be when he returns to Allah and he has in his possession that which he has not benefited the ummah with?"

Then he fell unconscious again and woke up. As recorded in Sahih AlBukhari, A'isha said, "We became concern with him and forgot to do by his order. So he woke up and reminded us. And we forgot to do by his order again due to the pain of taking care of him and he would reminded us again." Until finally they give this as a charity in the way of Allah.

In the final night, the brother of A'isha comes in. In his hands is a new siwak. A'isha said, "At that time the Prophet was unable to speak, but I could see him looking toward the siwak. So I asked him, 'Do you wish for it?'" Then she took it from her brother. She said, "I moisten it in my mouth and gave it to him. After he brushed his teeth, I took it and I brushed my teeth. That was the last time that my saliva and his meet."

On that day, the Prophet [peace and blessings be upon him] looked toward the heaven and he pointed with his hand while saying, "Rather I choose the place of the highest of people." Then his hand fell upon his chest. At that time, A'isha [may Allah be pleased with her] had him held in her arms, between her neck and her breast. That was the final words of the Prophet [peace and blessings be upon him].

Immediately at that moment, A'isha unable to control herself. She screamed. Abu Bakar and Ali entered. They saw that Prophet Muhammad [peace and blessings be upon him] had gone on to the next world, returned to his Maker. They laid him on his bed and covered his face. Then they exited the mosque to inform the people the death of Prophet Muhammad [peace and blessings be upon him].

On that day, due to the excessive weeping of the people, the city could be felt to shake. In that moment, we hear different commotion and different statements from different people. Umar ibn AlKhattab pulling his sword out and saying, "The one who said Muhammad has died, I shall bring his life to an end! It is inconceivable that Muhammad would depart us and died. Verily he has gone to visit his Lord as Musa has done, and he shall return and he shall order me to strike down those who lied about him in this way."

Ali [may Allah be pleased with him] was immobilized. He sat on the ground, unable to carry his own weight. Uthman ibn Affan [may Allah be pleased with him] became silent. He could not speak, he became dumbfounded. One of the men of Ansar who had just recently saw the Prophet [peace and blessings be upon him] heard the news of the passing of the Prophet, then he said, "O Allah, take back to you my sight so that I see no one after the sight of Rasulullah." In that moment, he was made blind.

All of these are authentically reported to us. The one individual who remained with his full composure and with his wisdom was Abu Bakar AsSiddiq [may

Allah be pleased with him]. In the midst of all of these, Abu Bakar stood upon the mimbar of the Prophet and said, "O people, come and gather around me! Leave off all of the others. The one who said Muhammad has died has spoken the truth. The one who worships Muhammad, let him know that Muhammad is dead. But the one who worships Allah, let him know that Allah is Living, Eternal, and shall never die."

The Prophet [peace and blessings be upon him] has given instruction that if he was to die, none was to pray over him. Rather, the Prophet [peace and blessings be upon him], none is worthy to lead the prayer upon him. The prayer for him were his dua. The ghusl of the Prophet was made with his clothes on. Ali [may Allah be pleased with him] would pour the water from on top of his clothes and rub him.

Abu Bakar entered upon the Prophet [peace and blessings be upon him] and uncovered his face. He then kissed him and told him, "You always were fragrant in your life and you are even more fragrant in your death."

All of the people of Madinah passed by the Prophet [peace and blessings be upon him] in his home, saying their dua for him. He had instructed that the nearest to him in family relations were the first to enter upon him. Then the first after them was to be Abu Bakar AsSiddiq, followed by Umar ibn AlKhattab, then Uthman ibn Affan [may Allah be pleased with them].

Fatimah, the daughter of the Prophet, asked the companions, "Did you have the heart to put the dirt upon the Messenger?" That was the time that the ummah received the greatest test. That is the time where even we today feel the sadness of the departure of Rasulullah. Who can not feel the sense of loss and not being able to witness the majesty and the honour of Muhammad [peace and blessings be upon him]?

However, that is the reality that we appreciate. That was the reason Prophet Muhammad would weak whenever there was a funeral ceremony.

CHAPTER 8

HIS UMMAH

In this authentic hadith by Abdullah ibn Amr ibn Al'As [may Allah be pleased with them] said that one day, the Prophet [peace and blessings be upon him] recited verses from surah Ibrahim, the translation says, "My Lord, indeed they have led astray many among the people; so whoever follows me, then he is of me; and whoever disobeys me, indeed You are (yet) Forgiving and Merciful. Our Lord, I have settled some of my descendants in uncultivated valley near Your sacred House, our Lord, that they may establish prayer; so make hearts among the people incline toward them and provide for them from the fruits that they might be grateful." Surah Ibrahim, verses 36-37.

The Prophet also recited the same of Isa [may Allah be pleased with him] as recorded in the Quran, surah Al-Maidah, verse 118, "If You should punish them, indeed they are Your servants; but if You forgive them, indeed it is You who is the Exalted in Might, the Wise." After reciting this verse, the Prophet raised his hand making dua to Allah. He said, "O Allah, my ummah! My ummah!" And he wept severely.

Allah Subhanahu wa Ta'ala said to Jibril, "O Jibril, go to Muhammad and ask him, 'What caused you to weep in this way?'" Jibril came to the Prophet and asked him, "What causes you to weep in this way?" The Prophet replied, "I weep because of my ummah! My ummah!" And Allah already known the reason of his weeping. Jibril returned to Allah with the information that Allah already knew. Allah then said to Jibril, "Go to Muhammad and say to him, 'O Muhammad, We will please you by giving you goodness in your ummah.'"

The ummah has been honoured with goodness and success due to the love of Allah for the Prophet [peace and blessings be upon him]. All of the happiness, success, guidance, and ease that we have been given as a nation of Islam is due to the love of Allah for the Messenger.

Look at how the Prophet [peace and blessings be upon him] cared for his ummah enough that even after reciting the verses from surah Ibrahim in his dua and the words of Isa in his dua, he would come back to remember his ummah. Look in the comparison between the words of Isa and the words of Muhammad. Isa is recorded in the Quran by saying, "O Allah, if You punish them, they are Your servants ..."

He did not intercede for his people and say "O Allah, forgive them." Instead, he say, "If You punish them, they are Your servant. And if You forgive them, You are The Most Wise and Knowledgeable." Meanwhile, Muhammad [peace and blessings be upon him] is the interceder, not just for his ummah, but for all of the ummah. When the people of Isa shall come to him on the Day of Judgement and say, "O Isa, make dua to save us", he will say, "Go to Muhammad." That is the greatness of our Prophet [peace and blessings be upon him]. His tears and weeping are out of love for his ummah.

There are few lessons we learn from this hadith. First, Prophet Muhammad [peace and blessings be upon him] is a person whose greatest ambitions in life were not for himself. He lived his life not for himself, but for his ummah. Everything that he did in his life was in pursuit of making things easy for his ummah. In the way he would answer the questions, in the way that he would advise, in the battle that he fought, in the defense he that performed, in the jihad that he stood up with; all of that was not out of personal benefit. Rather, it was for the fulfilment of the laws of Allah for the ummah of Islam.

Second, it is recommended for the believer when he is in need of asking Allah for something that is personal to himself or for the ummah, to raise his hand in dua. It is from the sunnah of the Prophet [peace and blessings be upon him] that when a person is in need and it is not for the time when one should not make dua to raise his hand and ask from Allah. This has been a constant sunnah of the Prophet. In an authentic hadith of Abu Daud, the Prophet said, "Allah would be shy from an individual who raises his hand to Allah in dua and Allah does not answer him. So raise your hand to Allah and have certainty that Allah will answer your dua."

Third, the success and rewards for the ummah is based on the love of Allah to the Prophet [peace and blessings be upon him]. It is very difficult for us to try to discuss the love that Allah has for Rasulullah. Let us look at some of the important ways in how Allah honoured Prophet Muhammad [peace and blessings be upon him]. Whenever Allah Subhanahu wa Ta'ala comes to address prophets and messengers in the Quran, he would address them directly. "Nuh, descend from the ship in peace", "Musa, throw down the staff that is in your hand", "Isa, I shall put you in a state of sleep and raise you up to the heavens as a protection for you", "And We call on to him, o Ibrahim, you have believed in the vision that you have seen". All of the prophets and messengers were simply given their first name at the address. But when we come to Muhammad [peace and blessings be upon him], we find nowhere in the Quran wherein Allah Subhanahu wa Ta'ala orders the Prophet with an action by calling his first name. It is always, "O the Messenger", "O the Prophet", "O one who is shaking", "O you who wraps himself", "A warner of the evil", "A caller to people to come to Allah".

The only time the Prophet [peace and blessings be upon him] is named is in reference of honour, in surah Al-Fath, verse 29. An honoured position that is not given to the others. What is greater in honour than to know as a synonym of the word of Allah, any time the word of Allah is mentioned, when you say "La ilaha illa Allah" immediately if you do not say it, someone will complete it for you "Muhammadan rasulullah". What is greater than in every parts of your salah there is some sort of reminder of the Prophet. Your salah is incomplete unless you say tahiyyat or salawat. What is greater than to know that Allah Subhanahu wa Ta'ala had described the Prophet in such detail in the books before Al-Quran. Allah describes Prophet Muhammad as being the one who would come and be honoured, the one who would come and have the words of Allah upon his tongue. All of these found in the Injil and the Taurah – that which remains, remains and that which have been removed, have been removed.

Fourth, the Prophet [peace and blessings be upon him] was not an insignificant being. He was the person who changed the course of humanity, by the will, the power, and the protection of Allah. What is greater than for Allah to choose Muhammad to be the final prophet of the final revelation of the final message to the ends of time of humanity. Nothing can be greater than Muhammad [peace and blessings be upon him] being given this mission and nothing was more difficult of a task than being the one who kept and fulfiled this task as the Messenger of Allah did.

Fifth, although he was in the lofty position and honoured status, the Prophet was also the most in need of Allah. As a human being, Muhammad [peace and blessings be upon him] is still seeking and turning and invoking Allah. Imagine him with the power wherein Allah sent Jibril said, "O Muhammad, for the people for having disobeyed you and having driven you out of your land of Makkah, here is with me the Angel of the Mountains. Order him and he will collapse the two mountains that surround Makkah upon each other and killed the people within its vicinity." But Muhammad [peace and blessings be upon him] with all his power given to him by Allah Subhanahu wa Ta'ala, he was equated in mercy and love for his ummah. He instead turned to Allah and said, "I ask you o Allah, to extract from within their people those who will come to the worship of Allah." That was the mercy of Rasulullah. That is what we seek to show to ourselves and to the people who we live with.

Sixth, with the Prophet [peace and blessings be upon him] invoking Allah by saying, "My ummah! My ummah!" it does not mean that the ummah has a safe passage through all times and through fitnah. Do not mistake this hadith for saying, "Then how come the ummah is going through all the difficulties they are facing? Why has there been death, hardship, lost of money, and lost of lives? Why is the ummah facing all of these if Allah said 'We will make you happy o Muhammad, in your ummah'? What this meant is that you are the answer of this dua of the Prophet. You sitting here more than 1400 years later, seeking to know him all your life – you are the answer of the dua of the Prophet. You gather with all different nationalities in unity in a mosque to worship Allah is the deliverance of the message of Rasulullah [peace and blessings be upon him].

"O mankind, indeed We have created you from male and female and made you peoples and tribes that you may know one another; indeed, the most noble of you in the sight of Allah is the most righteous of you; indeed, Allah is Knowing and Acquainted." Surah Al-Hujurat, verse 13.

Nothing elevates you above anyone else except your piety. Remember that the dua of the Prophet does not guarantee that you be secured from harm or difficulty or low income or excessive income. Sometimes we are tested by being given good and ease. That is more difficult of a test for us by Allah than

Allah to take it from us. Because you begin to forget your duties to Allah. Therefore the Prophet [peace and blessings be upon him] has reminded us, "If you see Allah giving a person everything he wants and at the same time you see that individual is in sin, know Allah is slowly going to bring him to punishment."

Allah Subhanahu wa Ta'ala describes the people who came before us. "So when they forgot that by which they had been reminded, We opened to them the doors of every (good) thing until, when they rejoiced in that which they were given, We seized them suddenly, and they were (then) in despair." Surah Al-An'am, verse 44.

We must be very careful with the way we conduct our life, especially when we have not received any difficulties in a while. The great scholars of Islam said, "We wait for the day Allah test us, so we know that Allah is loving to us." The one who is not given this test every so often, it means Allah is piling up until the final day or until he receives something great. Therefore we see the Prophet's dua is very significant to us. It is always important for us to look at his dua not just what he said, but why. From his often dua is:

O Allah, we ask for iman that is not rejected by You, and happiness that does not end, and things that will please us. (The companions added: And that we will be gathered with Rasulullah in Jannatul Na'im).

These are among the greatest things that affect the ummah of the Prophet [peace and blessings be upon him]. We are constant in remembering the Prophet because he is the key towards Allah Subhanahu wa Ta'ala.

CHAPTER 9

HIS MOTHER

From Abu Hurairah [may Allah be pleased with him], he narrated, "The Prophet [peace and blessings be upon him] paid a visit to the grave site of his mother. He immediately began to weep and his weeping had the effect that those who went to the graveyard were also compelled and felt the need to weep along with him. Then he said, 'I ask permission from my Lord that I seek forgiveness for my mother's transgression before Islam had been revealed to me. She was unaware of the religion. So I make dua to Allah to allow me permission to seek forgiveness for my mother and Allah forbade me from doing so. Allah would not allow me to make istighfar for my mother. But I asked Allah of whether I was allowed to visit her graveyard or not, and that was allowed for me. Therefore, I allow you to visit graveyards for it reminds you of the time where you will depart from this worldly life.'" Hadith recorded by Imam Muslim, Imam Abu Daud, Imam Ahmad, Imam AnNasai, Ibn Abi Shaybah, and many hadith scholars.

This is a profound hadith. In it are many lessons for the ummah in regards to the relationship of the son to his parents, how a Muslim conducts himself at the graveyard, and lesson on permissibility and things that are impermissible.

First lesson is that the Prophet's father and mother were not given an insured salvation simply because they were the parents of the Prophet. This is a very important concept for us as Muslim to believe. Allah Subhanahu wa Ta'ala tells us in many places in the Quran: On the Day of Judgement, there is no such a thing as blood ties or blood lineage.

Everything is cut and all that will be established is the piety of each individual. It no longer matter who your son is or who your daughter is. This lesson is taught to us by the Prophet [peace and blessings be upon him] in this indirect manner to show us that even his family were not granted protection simply because they were in lineage with him.

The majority of the elders and the tribal leaders of the Prophet [peace and blessings be upon him] rejected him. His paternal uncles were among the first to reject him. Those who were nearest to him, in his innermost circle of family were the same who disavowed him and kept their distance from him. Those who embraced his dawah and who eventually would become closer to him than any bloodline could be were those who were the weaker of the people, who were not from his tribe, who were former slaves or current slaves at his time.

But how is it that Aminah, the mother of the Prophet [peace and blessings be upon him] she would not be guaranteed salvation by Allah Subhanahu wa Ta'ala? The same question we would ask in regards to Ibrahim [peace be upon him]. The father of Ibrahim was also among the first person in his life, after hearing the statement of his son and knowing of the truth that his son had come to, rejected his son. Do not be surprise when you hear the story of Nuh [peace be upon him]. His wife and his son – those who lived with him, whom he enjoyed company with – were also from the rejected. Do not be surprise when you hear the story of Lut [peace be upon him] and how his wife, Khanata. She was from those who performed treachery.

Therefore, the family lines or bloodlines were never the basis of guidance. This is why Allah Subhanahu wa Ta'ala admonishes the Prophet [peace and blessings be upon him] and admonishes the ummah in this regard by saying, "You cannot ensure guidance simply because you have love for an individual."

Second, the obedience of the Prophet [peace and blessings be upon him] to Allah. The Prophet's mother passed away when he was at a very early age. He was orphan by his father before his birth and orphan by his mother before he reach an age where he could take care of himself.

When Aminah passed away, she left him as a young child in the guardianship of Abdul Muttalib and the rest of the family members. The Prophet had a longing to see his mother and had wanted to express his love to his mother in different ways. One of the ways was if he was granted the permission by Allah to ask Allah for forgiveness for his mother, she would be guaranteed Jannah and therefore would be in his companionship on the Day of Judgement.

However, in this hadith, when the Prophet [peace and blessings be upon him] visited the graveyard, he began to weep. He began to weep not out of pity for his mother or out of regret that he was not able to be of salvation for her. He began to weep out of his conviction in Allah Subhanahu wa Ta'ala.

He wept for his mother because he wished for her to have lived to see the day where she could believe in him. Not that he wanted her companionship. Not that he wanted to have the days that he had missed. But he wished that she would have live so that she would have an opportunity to enter into the faith that Allah Subhanahu wa Ta'ala had chosen for him.

"It is not for the Prophet and those who have believed to ask for forgiveness for the polytheists, even if they were relatives, after it has become clear to them that they are companions of Hellfire." Surah At-Tawbah, verse 113.

Abdullah ibn Abbas commented this verse by saying, "Before this verse came down, the Prophet and the Muslim at the time of the Prophet would ask Allah to forgive their forefathers and the people who passed away while in shirk. When this verse was revealed by Allah, they refused to make istighfar for these people who had passed away in jahiliyah. There is no prohibition for an individual to ask Allah to forgive and to guide the parents or the family or anyone else to the way of Islam, as long as they still have life."

Allah give us the example of Ibrahim [peace be upon him]. In surah At-Taubah, verse 114, Allah says, "And the request of forgiveness of Ibrahim for his father was only because of a promise he had made to him; but when it became apparent to Ibrahim that his father was an enemy to Allah, he disassociated himself from him; indeed was Ibrahim compassionate and patient."

In surah Maryam, verse 47, "(Ibrahim) said, 'Peace will be upon you; I will ask forgiveness for you of my Lord; indeed He is ever gracious to me.'"

The fiqh matter can also be extracted from this hadith. Is it permissible for a Muslim to go visit the graveyard of a non-Muslim? The answer is yes. The Prophet [peace and blessings be upon him] said, "I asked my Lord if I can visit the grave. It was permitted." Why is it permitted to visit the graveyards – Muslim or non-Muslim? We visit the graveyards because from the visit, we are reminded of our eventual return to Allah Subhanahu wa Ta'ala. Eventually, you will depart from this worldly life and you have nothing of success except your righteous deeds.

This incident in the hadith occurred during the later part of the Prophet's life. It was not while he was still in Makkah. In fact, it was within the last three or four years of his life.

This hadith also shows us that the Prophet did not put a great emphasis on things that he did not have power to change. He was constantly working day in and day out and always busy with the most important things. Therefore the issue in this hadith is meant for education of the ummah and as a way of him to relief the pressure that was upon him.

CHAPTER 10

SA'AD IBN UBADAH

The son of Umar ibn AlKhattab, Abdullah ibn Umar [may Allah be pleased with them] narrated, "Sa'ad ibn Ubadah complained of illness. Immediately when hearing that Sa'ad was ill, the Prophet [peace and blessings be upon him] went to him with Abdurrahman ibn Auf (one of the leaders of the Muhajirin), Sa'ad ibn Abi Waqqas, and Abdullah ibn Mas'ud. When the Prophet entered upon Sa'ad, he saw that he was in the stupor of death. Sa'ad was unconscious. That scared the Prophet to the point that he said, 'Has he already passed away? I was not in time to come and sit with him before his death?' 'No, Messenger of Allah, he is still living.'

"Immediately upon seeing him, the Prophet began to weep. When the companions who were with him saw him weeping, they were also affected until they began to weep too. The Prophet said to them, 'Have you not heard of what I have told you before? Allah will not punish you for the tears that flow out of your eyes and He will not hold you to account for the sorrow that you have in your heart at the departure of an individual, but instead Allah will hold you to account for what you utter with this.' He pointed to his tongue." Hadith recorded by Imam AlBukhari and Imam Muslim.

It is important to know that Sa'ad ibn Ubadah was among the first 70 people of Madinah who went to Al'Aqabah to take the bai'ah with the Prophet.

Sa'ad ibn Ubadah was an extremely generous individual. To put it in perspective, we know that the richest people in Madinah, when it was time after Maghrib prayer and they were returning to their homes to have the meal, some of them will take another companion with them to eat. Others would take two and three of them to eat. Sa'ad ibn Ubadah on daily basis took home 18 companions with him to eat. That was the generosity of this great companion.

Sa'ad ibn Ubadah was also the main provider of sustenance to the home of Prophet Muhammad [peace and blessings be upon him]. Everyday he would send a tray of food to the home of the Prophet. If he did not find the Prophet at one home, he would send it to each of his homes until he has found where the Prophet happened to be.

Sa'ad ibn Ubadah was a person who was very skilled in the archery and martial arts. He has a great courage. Anas ibn Malik [may Allah be pleased with him] said that one day, the Prophet and companions heard of an invading force of the Mushrikin coming toward Madinah. When the Prophet came into Madinah, he said to the Ansar, "I will only request of you to defend Islam if the Mushrikin enter into your city. I do not ask you to come out of your city to do battle. But you remain in your city as you are, until the Mushrikin come." Sa'ad ibn Ubadah was from the Ansar. He said, "We will go out with you and if you were to ask us to ride the waves, we would ride them with you." It means that not just we will come out of Madinah into the desert to fight, but we will also leave the desert and go to the ocean if you order us.

Sa'ad ibn Ubadah was a person which the Arabs would describe as literate. He was of the few Arabs of that time who knew how to read and write. That was a prized skill that all of the Arabs value. He was not just someone who had strength or class or power, but he knew how to read, write, and defend himself, other than he was generous and wealthy.

Another quality of Sa'ad ibn Ubadah is that he was able to swim. If any of you have these four characteristics like Sa'ad ibn Ubadah; generous, skilled in martial arts, literate, and a swimmer; then they will consider you as a complete man.

Muhammad ibn Sirin said, "The poor people of Madinah would sit a street between the time of prayers, hoping any of the companions on their way to the mosque would bring them to eat. Sa'ad ibn Ubadah would send to them people to tell them 'Come to my home'. He would not wait for someone to approach him and say 'May I come and be your guest at home today?' Instead, he was the one who made the invitation to them as a way of honouring them towards Islam."

In this hadith by Abdullah ibn Umar, we find many great lessons. First, The Prophet [peace and blessings be upon him] did not treat Sa'ad ibn Ubadah like any ordinary man because he was not an ordinary man. When you have an elder in your community, there is no shame for the community itself to feel the need to go and represent itself to him. Everyone has a place that Allah has given to them and everyone is deserving of being given an honour and due status.

The Prophet [peace and blessings be upon him] took with him the heads of the Muhajirin – Abdurrahman ibn Auf, Sa'ad ibn Abi Waqqas, Abdullah ibn Mas'ud – to visit this head man of the Ansar.

Second, there is nothing wrong of asking question in this time. What is the illnes? Has he passed away? What has caused this illness? The Prophet [peace and blessings be upon him] entered and asked "Has he died?" It is the right for the individual to know so that you can make dua to Allah to protect this person.

Third, weeping for an individual is part of your dua. Having this mercy and affection for an individual who is in the state of lack of health and in the state of death is a sign to them that you love them and that you wish for them success in the dunya and success into the passing of akhirah. When the Prophet went to visit anyone who are in the state of death, he would be in the solemn, humble state. It is not the time of joy; it is the time where we turn to Allah Subhanahu wa Ta'ala with sincere dua for this individual.

CHAPTER 11

REMEMBRANCE OF DEATH

From AlBara ibn Azib, he said, "We were in the companionship of the Prophet [peace and blessings be upon him] on our way to bury an individual in the funeral session. As we came to the place of burial, the Prophet sat at the edge of the grave. He wept and wept until the ground near him became wet from his tears. Then he said, 'My brothers, those of you who have faith for a similar day like this will come to you, be prepared. Prepare yourself for the day that is similar to this where others will open the grave for you and you will be immobilize and you will be at the mercy of others." Hasan hadith recorded by Imam AlBukhari, Ahmad, and Imam Ibn Majah,

Some of the scholars of Islam extracts numerous benefits from this hadith. When a believer is in the reminder or remembrance that there will be the day they will pass away, or when a believer goes to carry a procession to the grave, or when a believer fulfils this type of deeds; he is blessed with three types of characteristics from Allah Subhanahu wa Ta'ala.

The first characteristic is he becomes quick in his repentance. He recognizes that if he does not repent for whatever bad deeds that he has performed and whatever sins that he has fallen into, he will be held accountable by Allah Subhanahu wa Ta'ala. When a person ponders about the Day of Judgement and what it brings and ponders upon his separation from this worldly life, he will rush to repentance.

The second characteristic is satisfaction in the heart. You become satisfy with the little. To know that you no longer need more and more is a sign of richness in the worldly life. A person is not eager to have more than what he actually needs. In fact, the scholars of Islam mentioned that all of the sins that involved materialistic gains, such as riba and usury, done by people as they seek only one thing: A life that is not meant for them. They wish to live outside their means.

The third characteristic is you become enthusiastic in your act of worship. You have a little bit more strength, a little bit more endurance, a little bit more consistency in the acts of worship.

On the other hand, if a person is neglectful of the time of his death, then he is chastised with three different types of ailments. The first is that he is neglectful of taubah. He thinks there is always tomorrow. This is part of the philosophy; there is always time, things are all structured by the clock, the news on television is always at a specific time, lunch hour is from 1 to 2, schools start at one time, everything is based around the process that is not centred around our worship of Allah, the students go to school and reminded of their classes by the bell, everything is very cyclical. But in Islam, it is always around the act of worship. Day begins with Alfajr and day ends with Isha. In between, there is work and devotional duties to Allah Subhanahu wa Ta'ala as well as duties to household.

When a person is neglectful of the time of his death, he finds himself unsatisfied with his life. If you were to ask many people – Muslims and non-Muslims – who are not really in touch with Allah, you will see that their number one concern is "I am not happy", "I wish I was happier", "I wish my life is better". There is always this concept of 'there is more out there'. Now the concept of the human existence is "How can I get more for less?" In Islam, it was never in this way. It is not how you can get more for less, it is always how you can contribute more towards Allah, Islam, and the society.

The third characteristic if a person is neglectful of the time of his death is he becomes less enthusiastic of the acts of worship. He is not constant in his worship of Allah. He feels that there are always be another year where he can come to worship Allah. If he does not go to hajj this year even if he has the money, "insha Allah, next year, brother" knowing that he is able and has the opportunity. But that is not the frame of reference that the Muslim uses in his day to day life.

CHAPTER 12

BATTLE OF BADR

The Battle of Badr was the place where the line and the sand was drawn between Muhammad [peace and blessings be upon him] and all those who opposed Islam. This battle saw the minority with strong faith, strong will, strong determination, but weak economic, political, social strength overcome an enemy that was not just double in strength but more than quadruple in strength.

This set the tone for the Muslims. After the Battle of Badr and success of the Muslim, we see that Islam began to spread rapidly. It has always been part of human nature that you want to be with the winners. You want to be with those who are successful. Not to say that when the Muslims are defeated or when the Muslims are in the position of weakness that they are not still winners in the estimation of Allah. But it has always been a part of human nature that when you are successful and mighty, to other people it appears that what you are upon is the truth and what is correct.

Therefore, the very first battle between the Muslim and the Mushrikin set the stage for the success of the Muslims. It gave those who already believed in Muhammad [peace and blessings be upon him] renewed strength and commitment knowing that now Allah was in their defence. It also showed those who were not yet entered into Islam that there was no time left to delay because Islam was the wave of the future. Islam was what will change the world and its policies and economics.

Umar ibn AlKhattab [may Allah be pleased with him] narrated, "When it was the day of Badr, the Prophet looked out of his tent and saw the Mushrikin assembling. And they were more than a thousand individuals. His companions, those who had come out in defence of him and in defence of Islam, they were a mere 319 individuals. Then he turned toward the qibla and raised his hands to the heavens and he began to invoke loudly to his Lord. By making the following invocation, 'O Allah, grant me that which You have promised me. O Allah, if You allow this small group of people who believe in You to perish, none will worship You on this earth after them.' If the Prophet [peace and blessings be upon him] was to be defeated, and if the Muslims were to be defeated, there would be no victory left for Islam. The Prophet would repeat this dua, facing the qibla, hands raising towards Allah to the point where his cloak that was upon his shoulders, fell off his shoulders.

Abu Bakar came to him in a hurry, he took his cloak and covered him once again. Abu Bakar stood immediately behind him and flanking him. Abu Bakar said to the Prophet, 'O the Prophet of Allah, as such we have seen how you were invoking Allah, do not worry, Allah shall give you what you have been asking and what He has promised you.'

Immediately upon this, Allah brought down and reveal the following verse in surah Al-Anfal verse 9, the translation says, "(Remember) when you asked help of your Lord, and He answered you, 'Indeed, I will reinforce you with a thousand from the angels, following one another.'"

Umar ibn AlKhattab explains, "Allah sent the angels as warriors for the battle."

Ibn Abbas said, "One of the Muslims who was in the battle lines is getting ready to face off against one of the Mushrikin. One of the Mushrikin is coming after the Muslim man, he hears the crack of a whip from somewhere above him and behind him. And he hears the sound of a battle-ready horse. So he looks towards the Mushrik and saw he was slashed with something and fell flat upon his face. The man turns the Mushrik over and sees that his nose has been split, his head has been slashed with what appear to be a slash of a whip. This man who was from the Ansar came and told the Prophet [peace and blessings be upon him] of what has just occurred and the Prophet said to him, 'You have been truth in what you said. That is the horse of an angel of the third heaven that Allah has sent for our protections.'

The number of Mushrikin who passed away is 70 and there were another 70 captives from the 1,000 men of strong army. The Muslims prevailed with the loss of only 14 of their sahabah." This authentic hadith was recorded by Imam Muslim and Imam Ahmad.

There are many important lessons from this profound hadith. First, Rasulullah [peace and blessings be upon him] being given revelation by Allah on a daily basis. For now, more than 13 or 14 years after the risalah, he has performed the hijrah, he is living in Madinah, and this time they are facing off towards the Mushrikin. Still, the Prophet [peace and blessings be upon him] is asking Allah for help. You would think that after day in and day out the Prophet [peace and blessings be upon him] witnessing the miraculous events that Allah has blessed him with, he would be sure that Allah will help. You would think to yourself '... In this Battle of Badr, the Prophet would be confident to say surely Allah will send those who will be in my aide and my help.'

However, in this hadith, the Prophet is mentioned to have raised his hands higher and higher towards the heavens, that even his cloak fell off his shoulders, seeking Allah, ensuring upon Allah, making dua to Allah out of need of assurance from Him. This is not due to the weakness of faith.

Many people in our time has misunderstood the concept of dua. It is not a sign of weakness of faith that you keep on asking Allah Subhanahu wa Ta'ala. Today we have been taught that once you have asked, it should be enough. But in fact with Allah, multiplicity in the request is a sign of your need to Allah.

Therefore, the multiplicity of our prayers not once a day, but five times a day. The multiplicity of reciting Al-Fatihah, which is the essence of our Islam.

Even with his great iman in Allah and even with his certainty, the Prophet continues asking Allah Subhanahu wa Ta'ala, in more unique and different ways for Allah to bless him with His help.

Second, the importance of having a good, intimate friend. In his weakest moment, the one who steadies the Prophet [peace and blessings be upon him], the one who places back his cloak upon his shoulders, the one who strengthen his heart, the one who shows that he believes in him is Abu Bakar [may Allah be pleased with him].

How important is Abu Bakar in each and every pivotal role of the Prophet? Abu Bakar was the companion of the Prophet before Islam. Abu Bakar was the first adult male to believe in Muhammad [peace and blessings be upon him]. Abu Bakar, after hearing just few statements from the Prophet in the very first days of Islam, goes in to the city of Makkah and returns with five individuals. Five individuals who entered into the faith of Islam not because they heard anything from Rasulullah, but because they heard it from Abu Bakar. Eventually, these five individuals will be counted from the ten whom the Prophet will give them bushra of entering Jannah. That was Abu Bakar.

He was the man behind Rasulullah [peace and blessings be upon him]. He was one of the reasons of success that Allah Subhanahu wa Ta'ala placed for the Prophet. He came back to the Prophet and with him was Uthman ibn Affan, who would later become the third khalifah of Islam, who would marry two of the daughters of the Prophet. That was the role of a friend.

We learn from this hadith that as Muslims, we must be very careful and choosy with who our greatest support in life are. That is the true meaning of Allah saying to you do not take from the Jews or Christian people as awliya. The word awliya does not mean friends. We are allowed to be friend with many people of many races, many colors, many religions. Allah does not hold you to account for being friends, showing love, being merciful, and being honest to those who do not wish to harm you or expel you from your homes or your lands, as Allah has said to us in the Quran.

Here Allah is telling you that the one who is waliyyun hamim is the closest to you, who knows your secrets, your faults, your successes, your failings.

That individual has to be the greatest of people in your estimation.

The Prophet [peace and blessings be upon him] says to us, "A person is upon the way of life of his best friend." You need to be very aware who you befriend. Who is your best of friends.

The person who is nearest to the Prophet [peace and blessings be upon him] is Abu Bakar AsSiddiq [may Allah be pleased with him] – the companion in the cave, the companion before Islam, the companion after Islam, the companion even in the grave site.

Third, the mode of dua of the Prophet [peace and blessings be upon him]. In turning to Allah in dua, the Prophet did not just make dua without earnest and without sincerity. He took the means that his dua is to be answered. He turned towards the qibla and raised his hands. He was first assured of the danger – he looked out of his tent. Then he asked Allah with sincerity. He linked the reason for success with the worship of Allah. He did not say, "O Allah, save us!" or "O Allah, give us power!" or "O Allah, return to us our land!" That was not his dua. His dua was "O Allah, give us life so we may worship you more!"

There is a huge difference between what we experience today and the way, mode, and life of Muhammad [peace and blessings be upon him]. We are now more convinced and more interested in pieces of land, in stones, and all of trees. Now our dua is towards "O Allah, return to us Bait AlMaqdis!" Why? Who will govern it? And with what laws? What will we contribute to it that is not already there?

The dua of the Prophet [peace and blessings be upon him] is a very systematic, precise dua. His dua to Allah is not "O Allah, return us to Makkah!" or "O Allah, give us victory over this Mushrikin and give us what they have". It is "O Allah, if we are not victorious, who will worship You?" The aim of the Prophet [peace and blessings be upon him] is the honouring of Allah.

Therefore, it is important for us as Muslims today to begin to separate the true realities of the matter from what is in fact it is that Allah wishes for us. What it is that Allah want us to seek of him.

Our dua for our brothers and sisters is not just that Allah spare their lives, give them success, and they have good health. The important dua that we make is that Allah Subhanahu wa Ta'ala blesses them with faith and to come and return to Allah's way.

Fourth, seeking help with Allah Subhanahu wa Ta'ala in the times of danger is of the most important attributes of the believer. Think to yourself and answer this question: When was the last time you cried out to Allah in need?

It is very rare in our times today. It is very rare that we see this attribute of taqwa and iman in our daily practice. It is a sign of the time that we live in. The realities that we should be experiencing are now seen as delusion. We are not interested in the true realities of Islam.

Thus it is important for us to recapture this essence and the spirit of Muhammad [peace and blessings be upon him]. Allah answers him in the Quran, "(Remember) when you asked help of your Lord, and He answered you, 'Indeed, I will reinforce you with a thousand from the angels, following one another.' And Allah made it not but good tidings and so that your hearts would be assured thereby; and victory is not but from Allah; indeed, Allah is Exalted in Might and Wise."

If the Prophet has been defeated on this day, who is to know that more than 1,400 years later we are here worshipping Allah upon the sunnah.

Abdullah ibn Abbas said that in this Battle of Badr, we also see the story of some of the Mushrikin, when they came into Islam later on, they began to tell the companions of what they saw on the day of Badr. They said, "We saw behind you a cloud as if it is descended. And we saw in it beasts of different colours and different sizes that were making noise and that were terrifying us." To the point that Abu Lahab when he was in the battle, as he came to Abdullah ibn Mas'ud, he saw what appear to be a large bull. Abu Lahab turned to run away from what was actually a small size man.

That was the type of madad that Allah Subhanahu wa Ta'ala had given to those who were successful.

Fifth, in this Battle of Badr, the Prophet [peace and blessings be upon him] was a Commander and the Spiritual Leader and the leader of an ummah. He was not just a person who was in seclusion, who was just sitting in his tent and making dua. This is just one part of the hadith, where you see the Prophet before the battle begins, asking Allah. What you find in other hadith is that the Prophet [peace and blessings be upon him] was in the midst of the battle. In the Battle of Badr, there were four individuals met their demise at the hands of the Prophet. You find that in the time of the Prophet [peace and blessings be upon him], in each battle he was an intrinsic member of those who were in the middle of the battle.

And this brings us to the story of Uhud.

CHAPTER 13

BATTLE OF UHUD

The Battle of Uhud is the day the Prophet [peace and blessings be upon him] suffering victory and defeat at the same time. It is surprising to use these words – you can be defeated in one sense but victorious in another.

The Battle of Uhud was the second battle after the Battle of Badr. The Mushrikin went back to Makkah lifting their wounds. Out of their 1,000 individuals, 140 of them were either killed or missing in action. 70 of them were killed, 70 of them were captured.

The Prophet [peace and blessings be upon him] ransomed the 70 who were captured. He made it as a condition that if they knew how to read and write and they taught 10 Muslims how to read and write, they would be set free without any ransom needing to be paid. If they did not know how to read and write, and their family paid the diah for the dead, then they would be allow to be set free and return to their people.

So the Mushrikin suffered a defeat from all sides. To the point that when they returned to Makkah, their women refused to share the same bed. Some of the women said, "You are not man enough. You do not have the right to be my companion anymore. How can you go and be defeated by those who are lesser than you? Those who do not have their own country or state or power or politics."

A woman like Hind – who would later entered into Islam – when she heard her father is dead at the hand of Hamza, she refused to be near her husband until Hamza would be brought to death. She hired an assassin – Wahsy, a man who was trained as a killer, who used to wrestle with lion, a slave that own by her. She told him, "If you are to murder Hamza on the next battle, I would set you free." This set the stage for the Battle of Uhud.

The Mushrikin now said, "Let us go with force to ensure that we will not suffer defeat again." Now they call all of the surrounding tribes and they brought together an army of 3,000 soldiers. In the 3,000 soldiers, they had 200 horsemen led by Khalid ibn AlWalid and another from the captains of their cavalry in Makkah.

They came at the next date towards Madinah AlMunawwarah. When the Prophet [peace and blessings be upon him] heard of the nearness of this army coming, he began to debate with the companions.

He said to them, "If we were to leave Madinah and go to fight them, we would be out in the open and they have numerous troops who would come and be able to have the ability to destroy us."

The Prophet's initial reaction was "Let us remain in Madinah and let us fight them in the street and the women can fight them from above our homes by throwing rocks at them." But some of those who were close to the Prophet from the Ansar asked him to go out in strength and face them.

Anas ibn Malik [may Allah be pleased with him] began the hadith by mentioning the most tragic part of the battle before mentioning the incidents that brought the difficulties to them. He said that the tooth of the Prophet [peace and blessings be upon him] was knocked out. One of his molar teeths. The Prophet was struck and he was cut open, to the point that his blood was flowing that he would have to every so often wipe the blood out of his face, so that he could see with his eyes clearly.

"On the day of Uhud, the teeth of the Prophet [peace and blessings be upon him] were broken and he was cut open. The blood would keep flowing out of his wound, covering his whole face, he would move the blood from his face with his hand, and would exclaim out loud, 'How can people have any success when they strike the face of their prophet and cause his face to be covered with blood? And all that he is doing is asking them to come to the worship of Allah.'" Authentic hadith recorded by Imam AlBukhari and Imam Muslim.

"Not for you, (o Muhammad, but for Allah) is the decision whether He should (cut them down) or forgive them or punish them, for indeed they are wrongdoers. And to Allah belongs whatever is in the heavens and whatever is on the earth; He forgives whom He wills and He punishes whom He wills; and Allah is Forgiving and Merciful." Surah Ali Imran, verses 128-129.

This was a very tough moment for the Prophet [peace and blessings be upon him]. It was the moment that was full of sorrow.

On hearing of the encampment of the Mushrikin outside the mountain of Uhud, which is very close to Madinah, the Prophet asked the companions what their opinion was. What do you think would be the battle strategy we should employ? Should we go and battle them in the open? Or remain within the city and face them in hand to hand combat?

The Prophet [peace and blessings be upon him] preferred that they would be within the streets and that the women would be above the homes, throwing rocks down at the people. But the head of the munafiqin, Abdullah ibn Ubay ibn Salul stood up and say, "No! We will go out with you, o Muhammad and defend you outside Madinah."

This was a very important event. In the Bai'ah Al'Aqabah when the Prophet first spoke to the people of Madinah for them to allow him to make hijrah to their city, he told them, "I only ask you to defend me and my Muhajirin if the Mushrikin invade your city. I do not ask you to come out of your city to fight. You remain in your city."

Now one of these people of Madinah said to the Prophet [peace and blessings be upon him] not to worry about the previous bai'ah and that they will come out of Madinah with the Prophet, to fight. The Prophet knew that with all of the Muhajirin and all of the new Muslims, he had no more than 700 able bodied men. But if Abdullah ibn Ubay ibn Salul and the Ansar came out with him, then he would have more than a thousand troops.

Thus when Abdullah ibn Ubay ibn Salul said that he would come, the Prophet [peace and blessings be upon him] stood up and he entered into his home and put on the garments and the armoury of the battle. At that moment, when he came out, the companions looked at him and they saw that he was ready for battle. They said, "Maybe we forced him to put on these clothes. Let us ask him one more time what he prefers."

One of the important lessons we learn here is that never is it befitting for a prophet of Allah to put on the battle gear and then take it off without Allah deciding the matter between Him and his enemies. Never is it of honour that a man is ready to do something and then changes his mind. That was the advice of the Prophet [peace and blessings be upon him].

He put on his garment, he ordered the companions to get ready, and they got on their clothing. Then he explained to them a dream that he had. In this hadith, the Prophet [peace and blessings be upon him] saw a dream that his sword had a crack on it. He saw three things in his dream. He saw that his sword had a crack that penetrated it but did not break it in half. And that there were a large amount of cattle that were being slaughtered. And that he would put his hand into a place that would give him security and it would shelter him from the rest of the world and the environments.

This was a very moving dream that the Prophet had. When they asked him to interpret it, the Prophet [peace and blessings be upon him] said, "As for the crack on my sword, it means that someone from my immediate, someone whom I love dearly, would meet his martyrdom." As for the cattle that were being slaughtered, it meant that some of the largest amount of companions would meet their death. And the area of his protection would be Madinah AlMunawwarah – he would return to it in security after having lost a valued member of his family and many of the companions who would be slaughtered as if they were cattle in the middle of this atmosphere.

After telling them his dream, the Prophet [peace and blessings be upon him] said, "I order you to have taqwa to Allah and I order you to be patient when things get very severe, when you are in the middle of the battle, wait and do with what only Allah has ordered you to do to defend yourself and to defend the sanctity of Islam."

When the Prophet set out with his army of 1,000 or more – including the people of Abdullah ibn Ubay ibn Salul – and they reached near the battle of Uhud, Abdullah ibn Ubay ibn Salul changed his mind. He said, "You go and fight. We had promised you only to fight if they came into Madinah. Since Uhud is not from our Madinah, you go and fight by yourself with your people." That has always been the strategies of those who had Islam as an enemy that they are very shifty in their principle and beliefs. This munafiqun continued, "If we actually thought that they were really be a large battle, we will return and help you."

Allah records this statement in the Quran that they were just saying this out of fear. No truth were found in his words. Even when the battle began, no one came from Madinah to help the Prophet [peace and blessings be upon him] from those individuals who had remained behind.

The stage was set for the Prophet [peace and blessings be upon him] in that time. It was a very traumatic experience. Only now his army has been cut by almost half. He no longer had the reinforcement that he thought. All that he had were ten horsemen in comparison of the 200 of the Mushrikin. He had close to 700 troops when the Mushrikin had over 3,300 and they came near the mountain of Uhud. The Prophet who was always full of certainty in Allah and who was always invoking Allah as he had done in the Battle of Badr, turned to some of the companions – those who were the bow and arrow – and said to them, "Stand on this mountain and never leave it even if you were to see birds fall from the heaven and pull us out of the ground. You remain here so that the Mushrikin do not flank us with their cavalry and come from our behind." That was the order of the Prophet [peace and blessings be upon him].

He placed for them that condition and the battle began. The Prophet [peace and blessings be upon him] and the companions in the beginning of the battle were on the victorious side and the Mushrikin turned, running.

On that day, the Mushrikin brought all of their women and they camped the women at a distance where they could see the battle. When the Muslims army defeated them, they ran to their women.

But at that moment, some of the archers whom the Prophet ordered not to move even if they see the birds plucking them from the ground, talked among themselves, "Let us partake in the spoils of war! We have defeated them already. Look! They ran away to their women!" The person whom the Prophet made as a captive upon them said, "Remain there, do not move!" But they did not obey. He was the only one who was left.

At that moment, Khalid ibn AlWalid took that as an advantage and used the cavalry to flank the Muslim army. So now they were being attacked from both sides. In the middle of this, the Prophet [peace and blessings be upon him] was cut off from the rest of the Muslim army. At the same time, the Mushrikin made a loud cry. "We have killed Muhammad! We have killed Muhammad!" They have lied.

Some of the companions believed it and they threw what was in their hands, sat down on the ground, weeping for what they thought was the death of Rasulullah [peace and blessings be upon him].

But in fact, the Prophet was cornered and all that remained with him were twelve individuals. These twelve individuals were those who lost their lives, except for the last one. Talhah ibn Ubaidillah was the final one of these twelve who in the defence of the Prophet [peace and blessings be upon him]. He lost the mobility of one arm and lost all of the fingers and thumb in another hand. Talhah ibn Ubaidillah is one of the ten who were given glad tidings of Jannah. He is also one of those Abu Bakar AsSiddiq came with to accept Islam after hearing the first revelation. In an authentic hadith recorded by Imam AlBukhari, Talhah ibn Ubaidillah said, "There is not a place on my body, not even my manhood except it had been pierced with a slash of sword on that day."

On that day, when there were only twelve, all of the Mushrikin began to encircle the Prophet. The Prophet [peace and blessings be upon him] would say, "Who from you twelve will go out and defence for me against them?" One of them would say, "I will!" The Prophet would send him and he would battle with them until he died. One after another they went to battle the Mushrikin, until the final one was Talhah ibn Ubaidillah. He went out and he kept on fighting. Talhah and the Prophet both fought the Mushrikin one after another, to the point the teeth of the Prophet were knocked out and his face was gashed, until finally Umar ibn AlKhattab and some of the other companions came in defence of the Prophet.

In this incident, there are numerous lessons. First, the Prophet [peace and blessings be upon him] is a mere mortal. He feels pain as we feel pain. But the difference between him and us is his certainty in faith with Allah Subhanahu wa Ta'ala. He was always unwavering in his faith. In other battles, the Prophet would stand on his horse with his sword drawn out saying in poetry,

> "I am Muhammad, it is no lie!
>
> I am Muhammad, it is no lie!
>
> I am the son of Abdul Muttalib.
>
> The one who wishes to battle me
>
> Here I am, waiting for him!"

That was the courage of Rasulullah [peace and blessings be upon him]. He was not just a mere person who sat in a tent, far from the battle, ruling from his chair. Instead, he was in the middle of the battle, hurt and harmed, given victory and at times tasting the sting of defeat.

Second, as the Prophet of Allah, he was willing to accept the advice of others. Even when it contradicted his advice. He is the one who does not speak out of his own opinion when it comes to matters of faith. When he gives a judgement in Islam, it is based on what Allah has revealed to him. But yet, when he heard of an enemy who was encamped outside Madinah, he gathered the Muslims in the mosque and asked them, "What do you had me do? Go out to battle or remain?" Even though he had said he wish to remain, some of them said no, let us go to battle them, he accepted their verdict. It shows the Prophet [peace and blessings be upon him] not a tyrant. Rather, when it came to matters of faith, the companions submitted themselves to him and when it came to matters of military, strategies, agriculture, planning, and economics, the Prophet would take the advice and he would give the final verdict with what he thought would be best.

Third, the Prophet [peace and blessings be upon him] was a man of power and success. Even after Abdullah ibn Ubay ibn Salul performed the act of treason, the Prophet could have easily said, "The reason we are going to battle the Mushrikin outside is because we were supported. But now they have returned, let us go to Madinah and wait for them there." But no, the Prophet mentioned to us that once he is ready for an action, he does not rest until it has been done. That is from the character of a true believer. When you have made a sincere intention for anything, put your trust in Allah. Whatever has been destined for you, you will not be able to escape it regardless of whatever you do.

Fourth, the Prophet [peace and blessings be upon him] was a brilliant military commander and strategist. He recognized immediately where the greatest danger was. He chose from the companions those who were most capable of defending it. He told the archers, "You stay here and defend us. Anytime someone comes around this mountain, you defend our back." He had insight into where defeat could come from. But it was due to those who did not follow the order of the Prophet that lost was the result.

Fifth, the orders of the Prophet [peace and blessings be upon him] are not just frivolous orders. Whatever the Prophet brings you, you take it. And whenever he prohibits upon you, you leave it.

"... and whatever the Messenger has given you, take; and what he has forbidden you, refrain from; and fear Allah, indeed Allah is severe in penalty." Surah Al-Hashr, verses 7.

The Prophet [peace and blessings be upon him] was very explicit in his words. There are many things he also explicit with us in. Everyday we are in different battles like Battle of Uhud. Everyday you and I have different struggle that we are struggling with. It could be our fulfilment of our obligations of salah, or of sadaqah, or of zakah, or of lowering our gaze, or of being modest, or of not being spent thrifty, or of not being stingy. There are many different battles like Battle of Uhud. And there is always advice that is given to us from the Prophet.

We must think of our lives as a battle. The great scholars of spirituality of Islam tell us that our worldly existence is a battle. We are always in battle with shaytan. And we always have a commander. The commander in our life is Muhammad [peace and blessings be upon him]. He is the one who orders us; who moves us from the right to the left; telling us what to do, what to touch, what to take, what to have, what to leave. Those of us who abstain from the order of Prophet Muhammad [peace and blessings be upon him], are those who suffer the similar type of defeat as was experienced by those who disobeyed the order on the day of Uhud.

Are we successful in the battle? It will depend on our measure and acceptance of the words, actions, deeds, orders, prohibitions of Rasulullah [peace and blessings be upon him].

Sixth, after this incident occurred and after what seemed to be a lost, the Prophet ordered Umar ibn AlKhattab to reply to the Mushrikin. When the companions and the Prophet retreated, they went up into the mountain, the Mushrikin said that they have defeated the Muslim – they wanted to hear that Muhammad was killed, but the Prophet did not answer them – he ordered Umar ibn AlKhattab to answer on his behalf and say, "A day we are victorious, and a day we are not victorious." The Mushrikin asked again, "Have we killed Muhammad? Why has not he answered us?" The Prophet said to Umar, as revealed in surah Ali Imran verse 140, "... and these days (of varying conditions), We alternate among the people so that Allah may make evident those who believe and (may) take to Himself from among you martyrs; and Allah does not like the wrongdoers."

"Muhammad is not but a messenger, (other) messengers have passed on before him; so if he was to die or be killed, would you turn back on your heels (to unbelief)? And he who turns back on his heels will never harm Allah at all; but Allah will reward the grateful." Surah Ali Imran, verse 144.

The companions learn an important lesson that it is not the person of Muhammad [peace and blessings be upon him] but it is the message of Rasulullah that is eternal. It is not the personality or the individual, but it is the message, the spirit, and the words of the Prophet that led the companions to success in the worldly life and in the akhirah.

CHAPTER 14

THE LIFE OF THE PROPHET

The Year of Sorrow

In this year, the Prophet [peace and blessings be upon him] experienced two very traumatic events. Although the scholars labelled this year as The Year of Sorrow, in the same time they also labelled the time as The Year of Happiness.

Why? Because in it the Prophet [peace and blessings be upon him] began to develop within himself – and by the orders of Allah – a new identity for Islam and a new identity for the believers.

Up until this time, we know for the thirteen years of the life of the Prophet [peace and blessings be upon him] in Makkah AlMukarramah, the Muslims were under stress. They were under suspicion, under severe torture – pain, sadness, physical abuse, economic abuse, not allowed from marrying the others, only allowed to live in certain district and areas in Makkah. The Muslims at the time of the Prophet were seemingly the weak and the feeble – they were either slaves or former slaves. Those who were in Islam who were still in slavery were punished twice for having believe in Muhammad.

In the midst of these, there occurred the Year of Sorrow. Within a single month, the Prophet's main protector and main aide – although he was a non-Muslim – his uncle, Abu Talib passed away. And in the same month, the greatest companion of the Prophet in his early days of Islam, Khadijah bint Khuwaylid – the wife of the Prophet, his backbone – also returned to Allah.

In it, the companions described the Prophet [peace and blessings be upon him] as being in a state of sorrow. Once the wife and the uncle of the Prophet passed away, the Mushrikin had free reign to attack him.

Abdullah ibn 'Amr reported that while the Prophet was in Makkah, the Mushrikin were sitting in the Hijr of Ibrahim discussing with each other. "We have not seen any people who would be more patient to a man like him than what we have been patient in. Muhammad has disgraced our forefathers. We were once a solid community of people, but now we have disbanded. Some of our children have left our faith and left our homes and follow him." As they were talking, the Prophet [peace and blessings be upon him] came to where Hajr Alaswad is found. As he passed by, they began to harm him.

The next day, they sat together and talked again. "We have discussed what has already happened from this individual and we have agreed upon on what we need to do. When he comes and he says something that you already know that you hate and you do not want to listen to, all of you must rush to him as if you are one individual and bring an end to his life."

The first of those who saw Muhammad [peace and blessings be upon him] and who stood up to attack him was Uqbah ibn Abi Muayt. He held the Prophet with his clothing and began to choke the Prophet under the shade of the Kaabah. Abu Bakar AsSiddiq saw the incident and he ran towards the Prophet. It was a point where the Prophet was losing his life. Abu Bakar separated them, striking at Uqbah ibn Abi Muayt and said, "Do you seek to bring an end to the life of an individual simply because he tells you to worship Allah?"

Asma bint Abu Bakar also narrated that when the Prophet would be in his prayers in the Kaabah, the Mushrikin would bring the internal organs of any carcass that they had slaughtered and they would pour them upon him while he was making sujood. All of these occurred during the time of the Year of Sorrow.

In this we learn important lessons. First, the more patience you have, the more Allah will test you to see if your patience will last. The more patience you show, the more difficult your test becomes. Luqman said to his son, "My son, I order you to establish all of the prayers, ask people to do what is good, forbid them from sin, and be patient for what will befall you."

Why should anything befall an individual who prays, who give dawah to people, who calls them and to forbid evil? Why should be harmed? Why should he needs to have patience? Because never has anyone come in the practice of righteousness except that Allah will test him to see if he is righteous. To see if he will be steadfast in his righteousness. Be patient and persevere in patience.

"Do people think that they will be left to say, 'We believe' and they will not be tried? But We have certainly tried those before them, and Allah will surely make evident those who are truthful, and He will surely make evident the liars." Surah Al-Ankabut, verses 2-3.

To be tested is one of the sunnan of prophethood. The Prophet [peace and blessings be upon him] said, "Those who are tested in the most severe ways and terms are the prophets of Allah. Then those who are closest to them in faith. A person is tested according to the level of his faith."

Do not think that all of the prophets of Allah were tested with adversity only. Some of the prophets of Allah were tested with kingdoms and rule. Daud [peace be upon him] was a king, a prophet, and a messenger. Sulaiman [peace be upon him] was a king, a prophet, and a messenger. He had in his power the ability to hear the ants, to control the winds, to get the jinn and make perfect his buildings and structures, to transfer things from long distance in a blink of an eye. That was a great test for Sulaiman. Others were tested by Allah by imprisonment. Such as Yunus in the belly of a large fish, and Yusuf was in the prison for a long time. Others were being prisoned by living in distance from their countries.

What you find that is unique about Muhammad [peace and blessings be upon him] is that all of the tests that were given to individual prophets were given to him. Because he is the greatest of the prophets. The Prophet [peace and blessings be upon him] was imprisoned, was given success and wealth, was given the power of Sulaiman but he rejected it. Reported in Sahih AlBukhari, one day in his prayer, a jinn came to attack him. The Prophet held him in his prayer. He said, "The only reason I did not take his life was because of the dua of my brother, Sulaiman (Give me a kingdom that no one else has)." Allah had given it to Muhammad [peace and blessings be upon him] but he refused it and let the jinn go.

The Prophet [peace and blessings be upon him] was given the beauty of Yusuf [peace be upon him]. The scholars comment that the Prophet said, "Yusuf was given half of all beauty of mankind." He was so beautiful that the women called him an angel. They were so taken by his beauty that they cut their own fingers when Yusuf walked into the room where they are cutting fruits. Muhammad [peace and blessings be upon him] was more beautiful than Yusuf. But he was given something that Yusuf not, and it was awe. The women would want to look at Yusuf, but for the Prophet, even the men would not be able to look directly at him. "He was like a full moon", "We have never seen anyone compared to him in his physical appearance", "His hand was softer than silk", "His sweat was more fragrant than the best of musk".

Second, the times of difficulties that we passed by make us stronger. If the Prophet [peace and blessings be upon him] and the sahabah were to lose hope in Allah, then the Muslim ummah would not be what it is today.

"Among the believers are men true to what they promised to Allah; among them is he who has fulfilled his vow (to the death), and among them is he who awaits (his chance); and they did not alter (the terms of their commitment) by any alteration. That Allah may reward the truthful for their truth and punish the hypocrites if He wills or accept their repentance; indeed Allah is ever Forgiving and Merciful." Surah Ah-Ahzab, verse 23-24.

Third, as much as we are in need of people, as much as the Prophet needed Abu Talib and Khadijah, and as much as we might think that we need others, we need safety, we need rest, we need security, and we need wealth; there is always be ability to do more with the power of Allah Subhanahu wa Ta'ala.

A Muslim never says, "This is as much as I can take". Whatever Allah tests you with, it means Allah knows you can withstand that burden. Allah will never put more on you than you can take. You already are assured by Allah that you are capable in belief, in ability, in strength, to pass through this fitnah. Nothing is ever too much for you in the dunya.

The greatest dua by the Prophet [peace and blessings be upon him] that we can remind ourselves at this moment is his dua: O Allah, do not make our fitnah in our faith and belief in You.

Taif

After the death of his uncle, Abu Talib, the Prophet said, "Now no one is wishing to enter into the faith. None of these honourable people of Makkah wish to listen. Even my uncle who I had hope to have enter, has passed away in shirk. Let me go to a neighbouring city – Taif."

The Prophet [peace and blessings be upon him] went to Taif. At that time, the city had three governors.

All three were brothers. One of the brothers was married to a woman from Quraish. While sitting with them, the Prophet said to them, "This is the faith of Islam that I practice. This is what I have been telling the people of Makkah."

After hearing to the Prophet, one of them said, "Out of all of people in Makkah, people in Taif, and people in Yathrib, Allah could not find anyone but you? Who are you, o Muhammad? What are your credentials? You are a man just like I am a man, you are from a tribe just like I am from a tribe, at least I am a ruler."

Another one said, "I will not speak with you about this matter ever again." The Prophet asked him why. He said, "Because if you have said the truth, then you will take my power. And if you have lied, Allah is going to destroy you. So either way, leave."

Subhanallah, that was the logic that they had. That was the concept that they answered the Prophet [peace and blessings be upon him] with. The Prophet never went to these people and said, "I will be your governor." All that he said to them, "Worship Allah." But they understood that the worship of Allah had conditions that are to be followed.

How did they harm the Prophet [peace and blessings be upon him]? They set out the boys and the people of insanity at the road side and they paraded the Prophet in between. And as he walked, they would throw stones and rubbish at him.

As the Prophet left, he turned to Allah Subhanahu wa Ta'ala in dua. The dua that the Prophet made here was answered in the form of Isra and Mi'raj. It was as if Allah is saying, "If the people of Makkah, the people of Taif, and the people of the earth will not accommodate you, come let Me accommodate you in the heavens for a few moments to solidify your belief."

In this initial stages of going to this people of Taif, he was going for nothing but to call them to the way of Islam. In the way they dealt with him with harshness, with evil intent, with malice in their heart; it was a way of Allah Subhanahu wa Ta'ala showing the Prophet "The matter is not within your hands. It does not matter how well you speak or how well you present your word ..."

What we learn here is "Give the message and what happens after you have given it is with Allah." The Prophet will be held accountable by Allah if he had not gone to Taif, Allah Subhanahu wa Ta'ala orders for us to move, to act, to practice; but does not order for us to receive the good or the bad as the outcomes from it.

CHAPTER 15

MAKKAH ALMUKARRAMAH

Abdullah ibn Abi said, "The Prophet stood on a small hilly slope ovelooking Makkah. He said, 'By Allah, you are the most blessed land. And you are the most loved piece of land for Allah, by Allah. Had I not been forced out of you, I would not have left you.'" This hadith recorded in Sahih by Imam Ahmad, Imam Tirmidhi.

Those were the moment for the Prophet [peace and blessings be upon him] turning away from Makkah towards his hijrah. Some of the other scholars of hadith are saying that the Prophet said these words when after the Conquest of Makkah, Allah ordered him to go back to Madinah. Based on this opinion of the hadith, the Prophet is saying, "If Allah had not ordered me to leave you, I would have remain with you. But Allah wish for me to return to Madinah." Either way, it is a very important lesson from the Prophet's life.

First, love of our homeland. We are not people of partisanship, we are not people who want to have a specific locality or specific races or colors. Instead, love for the homeland is love of the land of tawheed, love of the land where Muslims are in authority, Muslims are in power, Muslims are in accommodation of one another. This is one of the points of evidence that Imam Al Alusi and other scholars have shown that a Muslim must have love for his origin, for the land where he is recognized for nothing else except his Islam.

In fact, when you study the fiqh of citizenship, there are two types of citizenship. There is *al-muwatana al-aamah*. To be citizenship of the Muslim land in general, just by having the belief as a Muslim. You do not need to stand up and take allegiance. Then there is *al-muwatana al-khasah*. The citizenship where it is qualified. This is for people who are non-Muslim, or for people who are Muslim who have just coming to the country. They must say, "When I come to this land that is ruled by the laws of Allah, I will follow the laws of Islam, I will follow the laws of the leader" as a way of showing our allegiance to the Prophet [peace and blessings be upon him].

Muslim have always value their homeland. Even the scholars of fiqh in this studies have always classified things as Darussalam (Abode of Peace) where we are at peace with one another; Darul Harb, where we are in the land where there is outside the realm of Islam – all of these are found in the study of fiqh.

From this hadith, we extract the love of the Prophet [peace and blessings be upon him] even if it was the time of paganism where he was driven out of Makkah, that was the best of land for Allah. Because that is what symbolize the tawheed of Allah.

We must have love for our culture, our people, our dress, our languages, our foods. It is important for us to teach our children love of everything that is associated to Islam. Our calligraphy, our art, our traditions, etc. All of these are things that make up the character of a believer, the identity of the Muslim.

Second, the Prophet [peace and blessings be upon him] was compelled to leave. It means Allah ordered the Prophet to the hijrah. Had not Allah ordered the Prophet to perform hijrah, he would not have left Makkah. The Prophet did not leave Makkah fleeing from the Mushrikin. He did not leave in retreat. He did not leave out of being kicked out. He did not leave out of fear they would killed him. He left because it is an injunction from Allah to him. Had not Allah ordered it, the Prophet would have remained in

Makkah, patient in seeking his reward with Allah.

Third, the Prophet [peace and blessings be upon him] refers to Makkah AlMukarramah as the best place on earth chosen by Allah. This is a very deep concept. Imam AlGhazali and some of other philosophers of Islam, for lack of better words written volumes about this concept. In this hadith, the Prophet [peace and blessings be upon him] was discussing a piece of land, rock, stones. All of us know that the Kaabah, as Umar ibn AlKhattab in a hadith recorded by Imam Muslim, when he comes to make hajj, he says to the people around him, "You are nothing more than a stone. Why do we call the Kaabah as Baitullah? It does not mean The House of Allah. It is a way of honouring the locality." In the same way we call Isa [peace be upon him] as *Rauhullah*. It is a way of showing Isa as being elevated by Allah Subhanahu wa Ta'ala. It is a way of saying that this is chosen by Allah.

The mosque is Baitullah. It is not where Allah resides. Allah is far higher in stature and magnificent than this. This is the House of Allah because it is the place we come to worship Allah. It is a place of honouring this building with Allah's name. No other reason. Therefore Makkah AlMukarramah is honoured for no other reason by the Prophet, except for the fact that in Makkah there is the first house where people drawn to worship Allah

"Indeed, the first House (of worship) established for mankind was that at Makkah – blessed and a guidance for the worlds. In it are clear signs (such as) the standing place of Ibrahim; and whoever enters it shall be safe; and (due) to Allah from the people is a pilgrimage to the House – for whoever is able to find thereto a way; but whoever disbelieves – then indeed, Allah is free from need of the worlds." Surah Ali Imran, verses 96-97.

The scholars have also debated which of the two cities is more honoured? Is Makkah greater in honour than Madinah? Or is Madinah more in honour than Makkah? Some of the scholars, such as Imam Malik, prefer Madinah AlMunawwarah because it was the abode chosen by the Prophet after the Conquest of Makkah. If Makkah is greater, the Prophet would have stayed in Makkah. That was the opinion of Imam Malik. But as stated in this hadith, Makkah is of great superiority.

Fourth, the Prophet's longing for the return to his homeland and his people. It was not simply that the Prophet [peace and blessings be upon him] wanted to return to be near the Kaabah or to be in this valley of Makkah. He wanted to return because the people he left are his family. He wanted to return with the tawheed to them, to show them the beauty of Islam, the love of Allah, the faith for Allah. For this reason, when the Prophet returned on the day of the Opening of Makkah, he brought around all of those who were Mushrikin. He said, "What do you think that I on this day would do to you?" They said, "You are an honourable brother." They were pleading for their life. They thought 'We drove him out of Makkah, we murdered the companions, we killed his uncle Hamza, we did this and that to him. He is now come with 10,000 troops and is invaded us. Surely he will slaughter us.'

The Prophet did not raise his head to look at them. "Go, for you are free." They were his people, his tribe. They were those whom he loved. From that moment, even those who had the harshest of heart, such as Hind and Abu Sufyan became the firsts to come to the Prophet and pledged themselves to him, seeing the honour that Allah has bestowed upon him.

"When the victory of Allah has come and the conquest,

and you see the people entering into the religion of Allah in multitudes,

Then exalt (him) with praise of your Lord and ask forgiveness of Him; indeed, He is ever Accepting of repentance."

Surah An-Nasr, verses 1-3

CHAPTER 16

A'ISHA BINT ABU BAKAR

A'isha [may Allah be pleased with her] was the most beloved person to the Prophet [peace and blessings be upon him]. In a direct hadith in Sahih Muslim, the Prophet was asked, "Who do you love the most from the people on this earth?"

He said, "A'isha."

"And who from the man?"

"Her father."

A'isha was a person who has a great place in the Prophet's heart. He loved her. He was a person who sought to accommodate her. He instructed her. Half of our faith in terms of the ahkam are taken from A'isha. She was a faqiha. She was of those sahabiyat who taught us the most about the life of Rasulullah [peace and blessings be upon him] that none of other companions could have appreciate. How he prayed at night, when he prayed at night, how his wudu was, how his ghusl was – all of these intimate details that we use in our day to day life, the sunnan are taken from A'isha [may Allah be pleased with her].

A'isha narrated, "Whenever Allah's Messenger [peace and blessings be upon him] intended to go on a journey, he would draw lots amongst his wives and would take with him the one upon whom the lot fell. During a Ghazwa of his, he drew lots amongst us and the lot fell upon me, and I proceeded with him after Allah had decreed the use of the veil by women. I was carried in a Howdah (on the camel) and dismounted while still in it. When Allah's Messenger [peace and blessings be upon him] was through with his Ghazwa and returned home, and we approached the city of Madinah, Allah's Messenger [peace and blessings be upon him] ordered us to proceed at night.

When the order of setting off was given, I walked till I was past the army to answer the call of nature. After finishing I returned (to the camp) to depart (with the others) and suddenly realized that my necklace over my chest was missing. So, I returned to look for it and was delayed because of that. The people who used to carry me on the camel, came to my Howdah and put it on the back of the camel, thinking that I was in it, as, at that time, women were light in weight, and thin and lean, and did not use to eat much. So, those people did not feel the difference in the heaviness of the Howdah while lifting it, and they put it over the camel. At that time I was a young lady. They set the camel moving and proceeded on.

I found my necklace after the army had gone, and came to their camp to find nobody. So, I went to the place where I used to stay, thinking that they would discover my absence and come back in my search. While in that state, I felt sleepy and slept. Safwan bin Mu'attal As-Sulami Adh-Dhakwani was behind the army and reached my abode in the morning.

When he saw a sleeping person, he came to me, and he used to see me before veiling. So, I got up when I heard him saying, "Inna lil-lah-wa inn a ilaihi rajiun (We are for Allah, and we will return to Him)." He made his camel knell down. He got down from his camel, and put his leg on the front legs of the camel and then I rode and sat over it. Safwan set out walking, leading the camel by the rope till we reached the army who had halted to take rest at midday.

Then whoever was meant for destruction, fell into destruction, (some people accused me falsely) and the leader of the false accusers was Abdullah bin Ubay bin Salul. After that we returned to Madina, and I became ill for one month while the people were spreading the forged statements of the false accusers. I was feeling during my ailment as if I were not receiving the usual kindness from the Prophet [peace and blessings be upon him] which I used to receive from him when I got sick. But he would come, greet and say, 'How is that (girl)?'

I did not know anything of what was going on till I recovered from my ailment and went out with Um Mistah to the Manasi where we used to answer the call of nature, and we used not to go to answer the call of nature except from night to night and that was before we had lavatories near to our houses. And this habit of ours was similar to the habit of the old 'Arabs in the open country (or away from houses).

So I and Um Mistah bint Ruhm went out walking. Um Mistah stumbled because of her long dress and on that she said, 'Let Mistah be ruined.' I said, 'You are saying a bad word. Why are you abusing a man who took part in (the battle of) Badr?' She said, 'O Hanata (you there) didn't you hear what they said?' Then she told me the rumours of the false accusers.

My sickness was aggravated, and when I returned home, Allah's Messenger [peace and blessings be upon him] came to me, and after greeting he said, 'How is that (girl)?' I requested him to allow me to go to my parents. I wanted then to be sure of the news through them. Allah's Messenger [peace and blessings be upon him] allowed me, and I went to my parents and asked my mother, 'What are the people talking about?' She said, 'O my daughter! Don't worry much about this matter. By Allah, never is there a charming woman loved by her husband who has other wives, but the women would forge false news about her.' I said, 'Glorified be Allah! Are the people really talking of this matter?' That night I kept on weeping and could not sleep till morning.

In the morning Allah's Messenger [peace and blessings be upon him] called Ali bin Abu Talib and Usama bin Zaid when he saw the Divine Inspiration delayed, to consul them about divorcing his wife (i.e. ʿAisha). Usama bin Zaid said what he knew of the good reputation of his wives and added, 'O Allah's Messenger [peace and blessings be upon him] Keep you wife, for, by Allah, we know nothing about her but good.' Ali bin Abu Talib said, 'O Allah's Messenger [peace and blessings be upon him]! Allah has no imposed restrictions on you, and there are many women other than she, yet you may ask the woman-servant who will tell you the truth.' On that Allah's Messenger [peace and blessings be upon him] called Buraira and said, 'O Burair, did you ever see anything which roused your suspicions about her?' Buraira said, 'No, by Allah Who has sent you with the Truth, I have never seen in her anything faulty except that she is a girl of immature age, who sometimes sleeps and leaves the dough for the goats to eat.'

On that day Allah's Messenger [peace and blessings be upon him] ascended the pulpit and requested that somebody support him in punishing Abdullah bin Ubay bin Salul. Allah's Apostle said, 'Who will support me to punish that person (`Abdullah bin Ubay bin Salul) who has hurt me by slandering the reputation of my family? By Allah, I know nothing about my family but good, and they have accused a person about whom I know nothing except good, and he never entered my house except in my company.'

Sa`d bin Mu`adh got up and said, 'O Allah's Messenger [peace and blessings be upon him]! by Allah, I will relieve you from him. If that man is from the tribe of the Aus, then we will chop his head off, and if he is from our brothers, the Khazraj, then order us, and we will fulfill your order.' On that Sa`d bin 'Ubada, the chief of the Khazraj and before this incident, he had been a pious man, got up, motivated by his zeal for his tribe and said, 'By Allah, you have told a lie; you cannot kill him, and you will never be able to kill him.' On that Usaid bin Al-Hadir got up and said (to Sa`d bin 'Ubada), 'By Allah! you are a liar. By Allah, we will kill him; and you are a hypocrite, defending the hypocrites.' On this the two tribes of Aus and Khazraj got excited and were about to fight each other, while Allah's Messenger [peace and blessings be upon him] was standing on the pulpit. He got down and quieted them till they became silent and he kept quiet.

On that day I kept on weeping so much so that neither did my tears stop, nor could I sleep. In the morning my parents were with me and I had wept for two nights and a day, till I thought my liver would burst from weeping. While they were sitting with me and I was weeping, an Ansari woman asked my permission to enter, and I allowed her to come in. She sat down and started weeping with me. While we were in this state, Allah's Messenger [peace and blessings be upon him] came and sat down and he had never sat with me since the day they forged the accusation. No revelation regarding my case came to him for a month. He recited Tashah-hud (i.e. None has the right to be worshipped but Allah and Muhammad is His Apostle) and then said, 'O ʿAisha! I have been informed such-and-such about you; if you are innocent, then Allah will soon reveal your innocence, and if you have committed a sin, then repent to Allah and ask Him to forgive you, for when a person confesses his sin and asks Allah for forgiveness, Allah accepts his repentance.'

When Allah's Messenger [peace and blessings be upon him] finished his speech my tears ceased completely and there remained not even a single drop of it. I requested my father to reply to Allah's Messenger [peace and blessings be upon him] on my behalf. My father said, By Allah, I do not know what to say to Allah's Messenger [peace and blessings be upon him].' I said to my mother, 'Talk to Allah's Messenger [peace and blessings be upon him] on my behalf.' She said, 'By Allah, I do not know what to say to Allah's Apostle. I was a young girl and did not have much knowledge of the Qur'an. I said, 'I know, by Allah, that you have listened to what people are saying and that has been planted in your minds and you have taken it as a truth. Now, if I told you that I am innocent and Allah knows that I am innocent, you would not believe me and if I confessed to you falsely that I am guilty, and Allah knows that I am innocent you would believe me. By Allah, I don't compare my situation with you except to the situation of Yusuf's father (i.e. Yaaqub) who said, 'So (for me) patience is most fitting against that which you assert and it is Allah (Alone) whose help can be sought.'

Then I turned to the other side of my bed hoping that Allah would prove my innocence. By Allah I never thought that Allah would reveal Divine Inspiration in my case, as I considered myself too inferior to be talked of in the Holy Qur'an. I had hoped that Allah's Messenger [peace and blessings be upon him] might have a dream in which Allah would prove my innocence. By Allah, Allah's Apostle had not got up and nobody had left the house before the

Divine Inspiration came to Allah's Apostle. So, there overtook him the same state which used to overtake him, (when he used to have, on being inspired divinely). He was sweating so much so that the drops of the sweat were dropping like pearls though it was a (cold) wintry day.

When that state of Allah's Messenger [peace and blessings be upon him] was over, he was smiling and the first word he said, `Aisha! Thank Allah, for Allah has declared your innocence.' My mother told me to go to Allah's Messenger [peace and blessings be upon him] . I replied, 'By Allah I will not go to him and will not thank but Allah.' So Allah revealed: "Verily! They who spread the slander are a gang among you . . ." (Surah An-Nur, verse 11)

When Allah gave the declaration of my innocence, Abu Bakar, who used to provide for Mistah bin Uthatha for he was his relative, said, 'By Allah, I will never provide Mistah with anything because of what he said about Aisha.' But Allah later revealed: -- "And let not those who are good and wealthy among you swear not to help their kinsmen, those in need and those who left their homes in Allah's Cause. Let them forgive and overlook. Do you not wish that Allah should forgive you? Verily! Allah is Oft-forgiving, Most Merciful." (Surah An-Nur, verse 22)

After that Abu Bakar said, 'Yes! By Allah! I like that Allah should forgive me,' and resumed helping Mistah whom he used to help before. Allah's Messenger [peace and blessings be upon him] also asked Zainab bint Jahsh (i.e. the Prophet's wife about me saying, 'What do you know and what did you see?' She replied, 'O Allah's Messenger [peace and blessings be upon him]! I refrain to claim hearing or seeing what I have not heard or seen. By Allah, I know nothing except goodness about Aisha." Aisha further added "Zainab was competing with me (in her beauty and the Prophet's love), yet Allah protected her (from being malicious), for she had piety." This hadith is reported in Sahih AlBukhari.

We can learn a lot of lessons from this hadith. First, it is permissible to have a lot – pull straws, flip a coin in those particular cases.

Second, it is permitted to mention an evil incident that has happened to you. A'isha speaks about something that was very intimate, very traumatic for her. But she mentions it as a warning to others. If there is a lesson for others, it is important for you to teach from it and to teach other people about the danger. Never just hide what has been a downfall in your life and think that it is something embarrassing, so you do not tell anyone. Rather, it is lesson that people learn from and it is one of the ways of the Prophet in teaching others.

Third, it is permitted for the Muslim sister to come and go as you pleases without asking permission. In this hadith, A'isha did not need to tell the Prophet about her movements during the journey. However, in this day and age, in certain places some people have become very stringent in certain things where they have no right. We know that a Muslim husband has a right over his wife and a Muslim wife has a right over her husband. But there is always this flexibility that is found in the faith of Islam. We have to understand that Allah has left things open within the parameters of the faith of Islam. The ummah is always ummah of balance.

Fourth, the amanah of A'isha. The Prophet had given her a necklace. The main reason she went to look for the necklace was later on as the commentators such as Imam Ibn Hajr explains that she saw this gift was given to her from the Prophet was an amana that he entrusted in her. Look at what she went through all because of seeking to protect something intimate that was given to her by the Prophet.

Fifth, whenever we are confronted with any musibah, not just at the time of death, always the first thing that we say "Innalillahi wa inna ilaihi raji'un". You lost something, you found something, you failed a test; anything it could be, recite this.

Sixth, the Muslim woman is to be guarding of her beauty if she notices someone watching. Alhamdulillah, the issue of Islam are very base on the usool of the deen. On the opinion of hijab, someone says you must cover your face, others say do not cover your face. But all of the scholars who say the Muslim sister does not need to cover her face and her hand, they say she must if she notices someone looking at her directly with intention of anything.

Seventh, helping an individual in need is a very noble task. It is important that we extract from this hadith that immediately upon seeing a person in need – it does not matter a man or a woman, dead or alive, Muslim or non-Muslim – it is a duty upon you as a believer in Allah to do what you are able to do in the help and in the defence of the individual. The example in this hadith is when Safwan did his best to help A'isha, while not asking many questions to her.

Eighth, a Muslim man is someone who is always very polite in his etiquette, always modest in his dealings and conducts with all the women he encounters.

Ninth, the action of the Prophet was evident to A'isha that there was something wrong. Even without telling A'isha that something was being said, she could tell just from his demeanour that there was an issue that needed to be settled. It is important for the Muslim husband and the Muslim wife to give each other signs of when something is wrong.

Tenth, when a person is ill, we do not compound his illness by informing him of other things that may be spoken of or said, or other problems. If someone is ill, it is better to let them recover and recuperate before we burden him with more burden.

Eleventh, the advantage of Ahlu Badr. When

A'isha first heard of the slander by Umm Mistah, she came to the defend of Mistah and said, "How could you say something about a person who fought in Badr? Those selected 317 individuals, the Prophet as narrated in Sahih AlBukhari, he said, "Allah looked down upon these people on that day of Badr and said to them 'Do whatever you wish, I will forgive it for you eventually'. That was the promise of Allah as a covenant with those who stood out in the Battle of Badr with the Prophet.

Twelfth, to search for evil news and to transmit it to others is worse than to be the originator. To be a person who hears something from someone and you be the link between that person who started the rumour and another person, the middle person is the worst of them. The Prophet said, "It is enough of a lie for an individual to transmit everything he hears." Just because someone says something, does not mean you have the right to say it to someone else.

Thirteenth, when a person act as a transmitter of other people's information, then he is in conspiracy with them even if it is unintentional.

Fourteenth, the sincerity of the companions.

When Sa'ad ibn Muadh stood up and said, "I will be the first of those to bring to death the one who has harmed you and your family, o Rasulullah" he meant it even if it is his own brother or sister. Because of their allegiance to the truth of the Prophet.

Fifteenth, in the most trying time is the time when shaytan has the most affect. When there is fitnah, that is when shaytan becomes the most powerful. When things and people are calm, shaytan is not in full affect.

Sixteenth, one of the greatest fitnah that is found in humanity and amongst the Muslims is that people fall into groups and partisans. That was never the way of the Prophet or the companions. On the day when Makkah was opened and the Muslims were victorious, the Prophet ordered Bilal to climb to the third storey of the Kaabah and to make adhan. As he is making adhan, one of the Mushrikin of Makkah, he looks up and he sees a dark skin man. He says, "Couldn't Muhammad find someone who is better than a dark skin person who looks like a crow?" That was the ignorant, the racism of these people. Immediately Allah brought down a verse from the Quran:

"O mankind, indeed We have created you from male and female and made you people and tribes that you may know one another; indeed, the most noble of you in the sight of Allah is the most righteous of you; indeed, Allah is Knowing and Acquainted." Surah Al-Hujurat, verse 13.

Seventeenth, burying the hardship with patience. For more than a month, the Prophet kept on hearing the slanders and rumours. Imagine for once, it was your daughter, your wife, or your son; just the first instance you hear, your first reaction is "Who said? What happened?! Let me see! Let me sort things out!" But on this hadith we see the Prophet, for one month nothing changed except A'isha said, "I did not feel the same level of tenderness." That was Rasulullah, a man of patience. He waited for her to get better, he waited for her to speak to him, he waited and ask other's opinion.

Eighteenth, the one who harmed the Prophet, whether by word or a statement, is someone (according to this hadith) who is worthy of being harmed himself. When the Prophet said, "Someone relief me from a man who has harmed me ..." that was understood by the companions that whoever harmed Muhammad [peace and blessings be upon him] in word, therefore he was worthy of the capital punishment. That was not contradicted by the Prophet. He did not say "no". Rather, the Prophet quelled the situation so that there would not be more trouble between Aus and Khazraj. The sanctity of Muhammad [peace and blessings be upon him] is paramount for the Muslims.

Nineteenth, the one who is elder, more knowledgeable of a situation should have more right to speak in it. When A'isha heard the Prophet saying "I have heard such and such .." instead of going to her mother, she went to her father first knowing the elevation of the status of her father. Thereafter she asked her mother.

Twenty, the example of Abu Bakar in this situation. Any father when he hears anything being said, the first instinct is to want to defend your children. Whenever we are in a situation, we only say what we know. There is no "I think", or "I heard", or "It could be", or "I supposed". It is only "I do not know". It shows the love of Abu Bakar for the Prophet and he had more love for the Prophet than his daughter.

Twenty one, any time there is difficulty; the greater the difficulty, the closer the ease. Even in the study of fiqh, when things become difficult and they close upon each other, they eventually widen. A'isha went from difficulty to difficulty to difficulty. When it came to the point that everything was overflowing and nothing else can be done, all she ever do – not even defend herself – was to say, "I leave it with Allah. I say to you what the father of Yusuf said."

Twenty two, it is more preferred to say someone is innocent than to say someone could be guilty. In our shariah, we are the one who have instituted "You are presume innocent until proven guilty".

Twenty three, we see in A'isha [may Allah be pleased with her] a true woman of understanding, even in her young age. In all of this, she was a true woman, true lady of faith, a person who has true faith in Allah. She said, "Even with all that have been said, I tell you Allah knows the truth. I do not need to defend myself." That has always been the principle of ahlus sunnah wal jamaah. You do not need to defend yourself when you are upon truth. Allah uncover the truth in the right time for the right reason.

Now we must ask this important question: Where is Safwan in all of this?

All of this hadith is talking about A'isha. How can no one went to Safwan and said to him, "Safwan, what happened?" Because in Islam, a person is innocent until there is proof that is established. The man in faith that we have is seen as not the person who is to be questioned. In fact, here we see an evidence that the testimony of one woman equals that of a 1,000 men. You have this false concept, some people will say in Islam the testimony of a man is equal to two women. In certain economic contract, yes. But here you see that what Safwan would say is not relevant. What is important is what A'isha wishes to say.

Twenty four, this incident was worthy of Allah addressing it in the Quran. When the mufassirin come and deal with these verses, they will always mention that the reason Allah recorded these verses is because this is one of the most often recurring theme in humanity.

Twenty five, the words from the mother of A'isha. She says to her, "A'isha, pay no attention to this. Whenever there is a charming woman who her husband loves her, people will always talk." Whenever there is an outstanding individual, people will always seek to bring about harm to him. It is due to the envy of the soul. Never rush to the judgement of anyone. Never rush to the defence of anyone.

www.ingramcontent.com/pod-product-compliance
Lightning Source LLC
Chambersburg PA
CBHW071608150726

48000CB00004B/1631